D0113692

# CONTENTS

◆

# Acknowledgments

◆

I'd like to thank fate for this book. Last fall my husband heard an offer he couldn't refuse, which in three weeks' time landed us in an extended-stay hotel for relocating professionals off a highway in West Des Moines, Iowa.

Feeling cooped up and in withdrawal after leaving Manhattan for midwestern plains, I found that writing about new life adventures, scintillating spa treatments, and spiritual awakenings was just the motivation I needed to start thinking about life's dramatic turns as bringing new options, new chances, new wishes, and, happily, new friends. Grateful thanks to Blake, Chris, Heidi, Hollie, Jay, Jill, Kathy, Metheny, and Michelle at Candlewood Suites in West Des Moines for their patient help with incoming faxes, phone calls, packages, and sense of order in disheveled times. Thanks to the many professionals at these vacation places for sharing their enthusiasm and their knowledge. Special thanks also to my editor, Monica Harris, for her talent and wonderful phone giggle.

To Elise Donner Smith I remain grateful for the thoughtful recommendation and words of encouragement. Other friends helped my work along tremendously by sharing their own spa experiences with me. Thanks to Patrice Littman

Nichols, Bobbi Kierstead, and my mom, Barbara Baji, a top-notch cub reporter. Most of all, I'd like to thank John and Lefty for their unwavering support. Their love makes me want to do things, and I'm grateful.

# INTRODUCTION

◆

Just how important is a vacation in the greater scheme of our lives? All too often, a vacation is the two weeks per year that we use to get away from the daily grind. Free from faxes, deadlines, car pools, and cubicle walls, we see vacation as a great escape. Without the physical confines—but still with the mindset—of our own realities, we can overexert ourselves on our travels just as much as we do on workdays. We can get stressed trying to find our way in a new city quickly, rushing to pack in more sights than is possible to enjoy. Or even worse, we can binge. We eat more (why not? it's vacation), spend more, and do less—all with the conviction that we deserve more out of life. Then when we get home, we deal with the consequences. It's enough to make us wish for another vacation just to get over our last one.

Well, we *do* deserve more. What follow are not "getaways" but 101 retreats in the fullest sense of the word. These are places to go for not only rest, but renewal. Places to draw a little closer to ourselves, to regain focus, a positive outlook, or a sense of inner peace. Places to learn healthy habits and raise our awareness of unhealthy ones. Places offering the settings, services, and feelings conducive to personal transformation.

These are the staging grounds for miracles. But you yourself hold the cure. All of these vacations are opportunities to work on your instinctual need for change. They intend to engage your senses, soul, and spirit in unforeseen ways to unprecedented ends. Some are restful; others are emotionally and physically challenging. Some ask you to spend time alone with yourself; others make social demands. All, however, pay off. The skills and knowledge you acquire and the insights or talents you discover on these travels will continue to impact your life long after vacation is over.

Perhaps the biggest obstacle to overcome before bringing about change, however, is our lack of direction. We want to go to a spa as we would a beautician and ask for a "makeover." We ask this without the foggiest idea of what it is we want to be made over to. The truth about our souls, though, is that we can't be anyone else. We can be improved, renewed, and refined and even start afresh, but the only way to do this is to draw closer to ourselves and to our true wants and needs.

The choices of paths you may take on your journey of self-discovery and renewal vary widely in terms of scope, experience, and expense. From luxurious spas to monastic cloisters, this book aims to represent the full range of new life choices. Some of the selections are well-known spas, while others are rooted in philosophies that can seem curious at first glance. Each deserves your open-minded consideration. We live in a time when East is truly meeting West. Modern medicine is beginning to embrace alternative methods of physical and mental healing. Psychologists are talking about the benefits of religious faith, and mainstream religions are taking a closer look into the spiritual practices that led a generation away to ashrams.

To encourage you to read through the options, all spas, retreats, and adventures are gathered according to our most elemental needs, in sections titled Earth, Fire, Water, and Air.

## WHY THE FOUR ELEMENTS?

This book is organized in a way to help you get back to the basics. Its four parts list vacations together that may appear to have little in common, but which in fact share the overriding influence of a particular element. Using the four elements as a guide, ask yourself what you want from your next vacation. Do you feel out of touch with your family, friends, and surroundings? If so, look to renewed contact with them in an earth vacation. Maybe you're lacking ambition, feeling physically sluggish, emotionally blocked, or stagnant in life? Then put some spark back into your step with a fire vacation. The more introspective water vacation can wash away your fears and physical inhibitors, reconnect you to your dreams, and help you realize hidden aspirations. If you can't dream—if your career and family have you harried, too focused on the outward appearance of things, and in dire need of some space to feel and think—then an air vacation may be more appropriate to free your mind and spirit. Only by addressing your elemental wants or needs, can these vacations make a difference in your life.

## HOW TO CHOOSE THE VACATION THAT IS RIGHT FOR YOU

Each chapter lays out a variety of possible experiences to reach general goals, only some of which will be suited to you. Price, location, size, and activities are provided to help you decide among destinations, but try not to let any one of these categories alone narrow your search. A spa that looks like a bargain may in fact add up to less than you hoped for, or more than you budgeted for, especially when services such as massage and treatments are à la carte. If you favor a spa for an activity or service listed, please note that these may be seasonal, for a fee, or offered in conjunction with certain programs only.

Size, too, can be deceiving, because many large spas and retreat centers offer an array of workshops with limited enrollment and an air of intimacy. Indeed it is often the larger facilities that have the resources and staff necessary to tailor their programs and services to the needs of individual guests. Custom vacations can be a real plus, or a real bust, depending on your personality type. For some, there's no substitute for the camaraderie and support of a group that works together to achieve the same or similar goals. Variety plays a part, too. One person desperate to lose weight, for instance, may prefer the empathic environment of being with others who share this concern; another may prosper by tackling a weight problem in the company of people fighting chronic conditions of different kinds. Diversity can make us feel less conspicuous, and sometimes point more clearly to the shared element of humanity in our own struggle.

Location can be the most limiting criterion of all and is the primary reason why this book does not organize its listings geographically. Take, for example, the case of a hardworking DC-area corporate climber who dreams of living smoke free. He or she may have the idea that a spa vacation requires the time and money to fly to Arizona for a few weeks, and so never turn to a page for "West Virginia"—where he or she could read about Coolfont Resort, which offers one of the best smoke-cessation programs in the country only a few hours' drive into the fresh air of the Appalachian Mountains. Midwesterners, too, may think they have to travel to either coast for their dream spa and wholly miss out on Vesta Center for Wholeness and Health Spa, which offers great holistic care just outside Milwaukee, Wisconsin.

The vacation for you should strike a balance. Hot spot or secluded sanctuary, luxurious in care or rustic in charm, your destination should, more than anything else, hold the promise of change and inspire you in just the right ratio of body: mind: spirit.

---

## SET SOME GOALS AND BE WILLING TO BE SURPRISED

A catchword among these vacations is holistic, which generally means that the experience is intended to benefit you as a whole person, including your physical, mental, emotional, and spiritual well-being. Because all aspects of life are interconnected, fitness, stress management, spa treatments, meditation, and reflection are not incompatible goals of the same vacation. As creatures of Western culture, however, we tend to be linear in our thinking, and may see better results if we set our sights on one aspect of ourselves we want to grow or change. Inevitably, as we approach that goal we'll begin to see its effects on other areas of our life.

Vacationers seeking to manage stress or find inspiration, for instance, may choose to learn meditation. Initially rewarded by a relaxed body and calmed mind, they can become motivated to make meditation a small part of their daily routine. The wide-ranging benefits of meditation as a discipline can include lowered blood pressure levels, reductions in chronic pain and anxiety, and increased intelligence-related performance.

Alternative medicine is another theme of these vacations. Many of us today feel distanced from our doctor. Our local

HMO can be too technical, impersonal, remote, and uncaring. The mind-body approach of a spa or wellness retreat can remind us of the importance of human connection and open up our minds and bodies to the full potential of acting on our own behalf.

---

## THE POSSIBILITIES

Whether it's a spiritual need, a problem with headaches, allergies, weight control, or quitting smoking you seek to tackle during a week away from the office, the program you choose to address a particular issue should have an educational component that goes beyond the outward symptom of distress. Programs for the chronically overweight, for instance, should address issues of self-esteem in addition to nutrition and exercise. The goal of any spa with a medical focus is not just to provide relief from a condition, but to teach new lifestyle habits or ways of thinking that can prevent this condition or other health problems from resurfacing. The sense of physical vitality gained on such a vacation can likewise awaken your senses, spark your wits, raise your ambitions, and invigorate your personal relationships.

If unthinking surrender to massage or other sensuous therapies is your idea of a spa vacation, don't be surprised if you learn or grow emotionally from the experience as well. Tightened muscles hold back the flow of feelings as much as they hinder physical movement. One of the benefits of massage is that it helps us pinpoint where and how we hold our tension. Knowing this can raise our awareness to the effects of emotions on our physical health. The power of touch is also an important thing to learn and share. Witness the many mental health counselors, ordained clergy, and avowed religious who now use bodywork to promote healing and renewal. The rise in massage workshops for couples or infant massage classes for mothers and their newborn children are also helping more and more people discover their own transformative powers.

Consider your needs. Are you craving the quiet of the country, or an outdoor adventure to muster strength or discipline? Are you seriously overweight, or are you just embarrassed or scared of putting more on? Do you need to let go and give in to pampering, or would you rather grab hold of the reins and regain control of your life? Is it a spiritual journey of introspection you're ready for? Or would you prefer the hustle and bustle of a conference-type atmosphere where people gather to meet new people and exchange ideas?

## WHAT NOT TO LOOK FOR

Since the goal is to embody change, you might want to look twice at a place visited primarily as a day spa or overnight getaway. While you can get some great insight and narrow in on areas of interest for personal growth at these places, you can't expect to effect lasting life change in a weekend. (Especially not if that hot weekend spot offers cable TV and nearby shopping as enticements for travel.) While some of the destinations listed here offer shorter stays, these are exceptional; they're intensive workshops of a limited focus, or sampler programs specially designed for New Age novices to learn the possibilities inherent in alternative ways of thinking, feeling, or living. Weekend workshop participants would be wise to experiment before spending their efforts, time, and money on a longer vacation. But expectations should be adjusted accordingly.

As a general guideline, you may also want to look careful-ly at destinations that advertise how their guests "keep coming back" four, five times, or even every year. Yes, time and repe-tition are a part of effecting change, and repeat visits are one way to reinforce new lifestyle patterns a few years down the road. But in many cases, pronouncements of this kind can be the sign of a quick-fix program, or a resort that dotes on its guests in such a way that it denies them the opportunity to learn how to take better care of themselves alone. The joy of a spa vacation can lie in its attentive staff, peaceful location, and exotic new therapies, but such vacations should also encourage the translation of reflections and discoveries made in the safe haven of the retreat to existence in the world at large. In other words, some educational component is necessary; we need the tools, skills, and sense of empowerment to bring all that we've learned or achieved home with us.

## HOW TO BRING IT BACK HOME

Books, tapes, videos, recipes, and spa products can put a com-mercial spin on any destination. As intrusive as these items may appear at your destination for serenity, taking them home can help you jog your memory of the spa experience and re-create it in another environment. People who start buying essential oils or facial lotions packaged with the name of a spa treatment learn to continue nurturing rituals in their own space. Later, they can experiment in concocting their own reju-venating potions off the shelves of their local grocery or health food store.

The surest way to bring out change, however, is to have support. Family or friends who understand your desire to change as well as your means to achieve it can be a bottomless reservoir of strength. Many spas or retreat centers encourage participants to come in twos, some in the way of discount packages for couples, friends, mothers and daughters, or fathers and sons. Bringing a friend or family member along is a great idea—if you each understand that some time alone is needed for reflection. You'll also need to agree beforehand that each person is free to engage in activities of their own choosing. This can be a hard thing to do if we are sensitive to each other's feelings. Sweat lodge ceremonies and vision quests in particular urge family members and spouses to participate in different retreat groups, because they don't want personal relationships to complicate the experience, or to get in the way of someone revealing feelings and aspirations in their entirety. This doesn't mean that the two of you can't go on vision quests at the same time, just not together. All travel companions would be wise to see the value of this approach when away on retreat. The greatest way to support one another is to leave your loved one some room for growth while at the same time demonstrating an interest in his or her pursuits.

---

## MAKE INQUIRIES

Write, fax, or call a destination yourself. If you've never been on a vacation like these before, maybe you know someone who has. (Or know someone who knows someone who has.) This book is intended as a guide, not a personal endorsement of every destination listed. Even in the case of places that I know through my own travels, I cannot account for the passage of time. Rates, rooms, and the availability of programs, facilities, and services are quoted here based on information available at press time.

# PART ONE

♦

# EARTH

*For the wood wakes, and you are
here for proof.*
—ROBERT FROST

# EARTH

◆

E arth vacations are elementally grounding. They're the optimal escape when we're feeling thrown off balance, directionless, anxious, overwhelmed by outside influences, or even isolated by depression.

It's a simple but important truth that life springs from and inevitably returns to the earth. Despite the relentlessly neutralizing efforts of fluorescent lights in the office, alarm clocks in our home, and climate-controlled heating and cooling systems everywhere we go, our bodies and minds remain connected to the earth's cycles. Our energies rise, peak, and fall with the rhythms of the day, the weeks of the month, the seasons, and the passing years.

But earth doesn't just cycle, it recycles. It's where everything comes together to take new form, and is therefore a natural source of power and ancient wisdom. Realizing our connection to a larger cycle on earth can, for instance, relieve us of the burden of needing to shape a unique identity in a competitive world. The earth's terrain in itself can illuminate the values of time, patience, and power. Viewing the eternal grandeur of a mountain or the vastness of a desert plain reminds us of our smallness in a way that is liberating: If the

3

world can't revolve around us, then neither can our own worries, fears, or perceived shortcomings seal our fates.

Finally, the earth nourishes us. From the fragrant gardens full of meaning to Islamic poets, to the harvests reaped in Old Testament verse, tilling the earth is universally synonymous with breaking new spiritual ground. As the fourth-century Saint Gregory of Nyssa expressed so well, a deep longing for change is in effect a desire for growth, for a "new heart like the earth, which drinks up the rain that falls on it and yields a rich harvest."

The following vacations aim to reconnect you with the earth. They can change your life at the most basic level — improving you physically and strengthening you emotionally. Many have activities that take place outside; others teach you healing ways to bring the outside in. Whether you choose a course on herbals, a mud bath, a hot-stone massage, a wilderness hike, or a week on a working farm, you'll find that encountering Mother Earth is a way to deepen your roots, uncover your true needs and goals, strengthen your resolve, and stand your ground more confidently. The purpose of earth vacations is not to come home wearing nothing but hemp, but to return with an awakened pleasure to be with the people, places, and things that make our home, our ground, a haven.

---

## BIRDWING SPA
### Litchfield, Minnesota

Birdwing is an upper midwestern center for life enhancement that focuses on physical exercise and soothing spa indulgences. The setting is the old Birdwing mansion, a majestic Tudor home overlooking Birdwing Bay. The landscape vistas are apt since the emphasis here is clearly on the outdoors, with a range of year-round activities such as cross-country skiing, hiking, canoeing, and biking. Indoor activity is not neglected, however. Birdwing features a well-equipped and spacious workout facility that also serves as a site for aerobics and yoga classes.

Center stage at Birdwing is its Image Salon, which offers a wide range of luxury pampering services during two daily Image Sessions. Treatments include Swedish and Esalen massage, facials, hair care, manicures, and aromatherapy, as well as fitness and nutritional counseling. After supper experts speak on topics relating to health, stress management, and nutrition. On a lighter note, there are also movies to watch and cooking classes to attend. The latter can be impromptu, since guests are also free to walk into the kitchen at any time and watch the chef prepare meals.

**Season**  Year-round.

**Environs**  Lakeside location in northern-plains farm country, 90 minutes north of Minneapolis–St. Paul.

**Accommodations**  Standard single and double rooms, including a barn Jacuzzi suite.

**Activities and Services**  Fitness center, Jacuzzi, sauna, outdoor swimming pool, canoeing on Star Lake, hiking, biking, and cross-country trails, snowshoeing. Massage, facials, various body treatments. Mountain bikes, snowshoes, cross-country skis, and canoes are provided.

**Religious Affiliation**  None.

**Rates**  Five-day stays range from $1,050 to $1,350; seven-day from $1,295 to $1,775.

**For More Information**  Birdwing Spa, 21398 575th Avenue, Litchfield, Minn. 55355; phone (320) 693-6064; fax (320) 693-7026; e-mail: birdwing@hutchtel.net; Website: www.birdwing-spa.com.

## CANYON RANCH
**Tucson, Arizona**

The desert foothills of the Santa Catalina Mountains are home to this mecca for seekers of better health and wellness. Consistently ranking at the top of lists by spa aficionados, Canyon Ranch continues to live up to its reputation as an innovator in the spa industry.

Canyon Ranch has grown a great deal over its twenty years of operation, but its single-story adobe cottages remain unassuming and in harmony with the surrounding south-western landscape. Its wide range of programs emphasizes health, fitness, life enhancement, and nutrition. So does your local gym, but here you'll never have a problem finding a trainer—the guest-to-staff ratio is nearly 3:1. The main spa is a virtual coliseum, measuring sixty-two thousand square feet. Inside is a lounge, an art gallery, seven gymnasiums, exercise and weight rooms, a squash court, three racquetball courts, a yoga and meditation dome, men's and women's locker rooms with sauna, steam, and inhalation rooms, whirlpools, and private sunbathing areas. This complex also houses the skin-care and beauty salons and massage, herbal, and hydromassage rooms. Nearby are seven lighted tennis courts and a basketball court, plus one indoor and three outdoor pools. Biking and hiking are also part of the Canyon Ranch scene, as well as a fully staffed golf school and an aquatic center with two aqua therapy pools, a whirlpool, an exercise pool, and three pools reserved for water shiatsu (Watsu).

The jewel in the ranch's crown, however, is its Life Enhancement Program, which operates out of a separate complex with its own spa and health center. Armed with six physicians, fifteen nurses, two behavioral doctors, and a slew of other medical professionals, the Life Enhancement Center can help you face specific health and wellness issues head-on. This is a structured and supportive setting for guests to quit smoking, lose weight, or cope with other sensitive health and longevity issues. The staff is attentive, but not doting, as the goal is to teach guests how to take care of themselves. Guests can learn to read their own medical charts, design an exercise or relaxation program to take home, and even learn to prepare Canyon Ranch's celebrated spa cuisine.

So vital a retreat for so many people, Canyon Ranch has thankfully opened another location across the country in the Berkshire Mountains of Massachusetts. Both are worth your visit.

**Season**    Year-round; the peak season is from October to mid-June.

**Environs**    A full-service spa resort on seventy acres of Arizona desert only thirty minutes from Tucson.

**Accommodations**    Private rooms in casitas and suites, or private cottages with kitchen and laundry; all have private bath, large beds, and year-round air conditioning. Three meals provided daily from an exceptional spa menu (vegetarians accommodated).

**Activities and Services**    Mountain biking and hiking, exercise classes and bodywork, indoor and outdoor pools, racquet sports, volleyball, and more. Spa treatments too numerous to mention (including fifteen types of massage, aromatherapy, and herbal wraps); nutritionist consultations, biofeedback program, cooking classes and much, much more.

**Religious Affiliation**    None.

**Rates**    Five-day/four-night standard packages average around $2,000, eight-day/seven-night around $3,000; two days payable in advance. There is a four-night minimum stay from mid-September to mid-June.

**For More Information**    Canyon Ranch, 8600 East Rockcliff Road, Tucson, Ariz. 85715; phone (800) 726-9900 or (520) 749-9000; fax (520) 749-7755; Website: www.canyonranch.com.

———————————

## CANYON RANCH IN THE BERKSHIRES
## Lenox, Massachusetts

This sister spa to Canyon Ranch in Tucson sits on 120 acres of prime forestland in the magnificent Berkshire Mountains of

western Massachusetts. The dining room, library, and Health and Healing Center are all found in Bellfontaine, a turn-of-the-century mansion that recalls a time when the wealthy sets from Boston and New York fled to the country from the grimy cities to summer in luxurious ease. Today, guests are housed in a modern New England–style inn with access to a one-hun-dred-thousand-square-foot spa complex. Massachusetts is no Arizona in the winter, so Canyon Ranch has wisely connected its three main buildings by glass-enclosed walkways. While there's no need to brave the frigid New England winter for a strenuous workout, activities such as cross-country skiing just may draw you outdoors regardless.

Dramatic changes of season are in fact what the Berkshire location has to offer Canyon Ranch fans. Unlike its sister spa in the desert, Canyon Ranch in the Berkshires offers a full range of outdoor activities to complement each time of year. In the summer months, it is also at the heart of one of the most active art centers in the country. The Tanglewood Music Festival is only minutes away, as are the dance concerts at Jacob's Pillow and theater at the Berkshire Theatre Festival.

Treatments available at the spa are as cutting-edge as the art colonies that surround it. Not all, but most of the spa services and classes beloved in Tucson are available here. Trainers and masseurs are happy to explain their craft. There are more than forty fitness classes daily and working up an appetite is recommended, since the food is exceptional. All in all, the Canyon Ranch philosophy that guests should be encouraged to make their own healthy and life-affirming choices is unchanged by geography.

**Season**   Year-round.

**Environs**   The Berkshire Mountains of western Massachusetts, about three hours from New York City and Boston.

**Accommodations**   Rooms and suites, all climate controlled and featuring modern hotel conveniences.

**Activities and Services**   High-tech gym, aerobics studios, free weights. Indoor and heated outdoor pool. Separate areas for men and women with sauna, steam rooms, and Jacuzzi. Wide range of spa treatments including herbal wraps, massage, aromatherapy, hydrotherapy, and acupuncture. Counseling available on nutrition and fitness.

**Religious Affiliation**   None.

**Rates**   Eight-day/seven-night per-person, double-occupancy rates range from $1,860 to $2,950; this includes three meals daily.

**For More Information**   Canyon Ranch in the Berkshires, 165 Kimball Street (Route 7A), Lenox, Mass. 01240; phone (800) 742-9000 or (413) 637-4100; Website: www.canyonranch.com.

## THE CLEARING
### Ellison Bay, Wisconsin

Jens Jensen, the famous Danish-born landscape architect, made a reputation in America using native plants and motifs in his environmental designs. He believed that people are profoundly affected by their environment and therefore advocated that gardens, parks, roads, and cityscapes be in harmony with nature and its ecological processes. Jensen's convictions became a major theme of modern American landscape design and a working principle of the Clearing, which he founded in 1935.

Jensen conceived of the Clearing—modeled after folk schools of his native Denmark—quite literally as a place for city dwellers to come and "clear" their minds. Through renewed contact with the soil and the experience of learning crafts and trades in a close-knit community, he hoped others could learn to value the human role in nature as well as their own contributions to it. Today Jensen's retreat continues its mission as both a place for contemplation and an adult school of discovery in the arts, nature, and humanities.

The Clearing offers four- and seven-day programs in the summer months and weekend programs in the fall. Many classes are held outdoors, and all tend to build a camaraderie reminiscent of summer camp (expect campfires and picnics). Topics of study vary from rest and relaxation techniques to nature studies, photography, writing, drama, and music. During the winter months, classes are attended primarily by Door County residents.

**Season** Summer and fall workshops for retreatants; winter classes are shorter in focus.

**Environs**   This secluded cluster of rustic buildings set on a high bluff in Wisconsin's scenic Door County overlooks Lake Michigan. Comprising 128 wooded acres, the Clearing is on the National Register of Historic Places. Its lodge and schoolhouse were designed by Jensen in collaboration with Hugh Garden. More buildings (including the dormitories) have been added, but all are constructed of log or native limestone in keeping with the setting.

**Accommodations**   Cabins and cottages (all listed on the National Register of Historic Places) shared by one to five guests. Bathrooms are modern; dining is family-style.

**Activities and Services**   T'ai chi and chi kung classes, art therapy, crafts, storytelling, dream catching, and nature workshops. Leisure activities include hiking, swimming, fishing, cycling, and campfire fun.

**Religious Affiliation**   None.

**Rates**   Seven-day classes average $570 (twin bed), or $530 (dorm); four-day classes are $372 (twin bed), or $346 (dorm); this includes program fees, room, and board.

**For More Information**   The Clearing, 12171 Garrett Bay Road, P.O. Box 65, Ellison Bay, Wis. 54210; phone (920) 854-4088; fax (920) 854-9751; e-mail: clearing@mail.wiscnet; Website: doorcounty.org/clearing/clearing.html.

---

## FOXHOLLOW LIFE ENRICHMENT AND WELLNESS CENTER
**Crestwood, Kentucky**

Foxhollow began as a converted hundred-year-old farm manor-house inn and retreat center, with adjacent guesthouse and cottages for overnight guests. In recent years the facilities and services at Foxhollow have expanded in number and breadth. Foxhollow's on-site full-service spa, the Wetlands, is now housed in another renovated farmhouse named for the surrounding environmentally registered wetlands.

The Wetlands offers relaxation therapies including various forms of massage and hydrotherapy. As for fitness and health in general at Foxhollow, guests can pursue physician-designed programs in anti-aging and rejuvenation, or programs addressing chronic issues such as stress, hypertension, and arthritis.

Exercise classes at Foxhollow include workouts with a personal trainer and traditional yoga forms as well as more innovative ones (Office Yoga, for example). Another specialty is pilates, a form of exercise involving more than five hundred free-form movements, many of which are performed on a specially designed low-weight-bearing apparatus. New and expectant mothers can get excited about pregnancy massage services and an infant massage workshop, a physically and spiritually powerful way to bond with your baby.

Other workshops address topics ranging from vegetarian cooking to food cravings and addictions, handling menopause naturally, and eliminating allergies through natural remedies. Spiritual offerings include pastoral counseling, guided imagery and life readings, and meditative strolls along scenic nature paths.

With a mission to achieve and maintain wellness through the body's own healing capabilities, a new Wellness Clinic (opened 1999) features state-of-the-art equipment, practitioners' areas for medical, dental, psychological, nutritional, and chiropractic assessments, a lecture hall, and a learning center to facilitate guests' research in their individual areas of interest. Foxhollow's Wellness Clinic works in affiliation with the Paracelsus Klinik of Lustmühle, Switzerland, a clinic in its fifth decade of operation that's recognized internationally for its role on the leading edge of biological medicine.

**Season**   Year-round.

**Environs**   Manor-house grounds consisting of thirteen hundred acres of rolling green Kentucky countryside, with streams, wetlands, nature trails, and woods; twenty minutes from downtown Louisville.

**Accommodations**   Single and double rooms in your choice of the manor house, guesthouse, farmer's house, carriage house, or two cottages. Meals are gourmet vegetarian.

**Activities and Services**   Physician-designed fitness programs, spa services including hydrotherapy and shiatsu/reflexology massage, personal fitness trainers, yoga and pilates classes, pool for swimming and tennis. Chiropractic treatments, nutritional consultations, and spiritual and pastoral counseling.

**Religious Affiliation**   None.

**Rates**   Rooms from $55 to $75, house rentals (three to four bedrooms, two bathrooms) from $160 to $300. Exercise classes $10 per session. Spa packages are available; otherwise all treatments are à la carte.

**For More Information**   Foxhollow Life Enrichment and Wellness Center, 8909 Highway 329, Crestwood, Ky. 40014; phone (800) 624-7080 or (502) 241-8621; fax (502) 241-3935; Website: www.Foxhollowus.com.

———————

FRENCH MEADOWS CAMP
**(The George Ohsawa Macrobiotic Foundation)
Oroville, California**

Those who follow the macrobiotic philosophy believe that healthy eating is simply the surest way to a happy life. But their philosophy is also a discipline requiring a solid understanding of the body's nutritional needs in order to be effective.

Every year, the George Ohsawa Macrobiotic Foundation (GOMF), a leading authority in macrobiotics since the early 1960s, hosts this retreat to raise awareness of and support for its work. Known as the annual French Meadows Camp, this ten-day event is held in the spectacular Tahoe National Forest. Participants can learn about the macrobiotic way of life while spending time in one of the most beautiful wilderness locales in North America.

A retreat in the classic sense, French Meadows brings experts and interested souls together and gives each a chance to learn from the other. The campground setting, with its majestic trees bordering streams and ancient rock formations, is ideal for learning the irreducible tenets of macrobiotic living; the daily meals, with their emphasis on grains and vegetables, are an introduction to the idea of nurturing and healing food.

**Season** Ten days in midsummer (in 1999, July 15–25).

**Environs** A campground retreat in the Tahoe National Forest.

**Accommodations** Campground facilities for tents, campers, or RVs. Participants must provide basic necessities. Meals and campground fees are included.

**Activities and Services** Lectures, consultations, and workshops hosted by leading speakers in the macrobiotic field. Waterfall hiking, campfire gatherings, volleyball, swimming.

**Religious Affiliation** None.

**Rates** GOMF members $500 ($550 late registration); nonmembers $550 ($600 late registration); youths (ages three to sixteen) $300 ($350 late registration).

**For More Information** GOMF Summer Camp, P.O. Box 426, Oroville, Calif. 95965; phone (800) 232-2372.

## GREEN MOUNTAIN AT FOX RUN
## Ludlow, Vermont

Green Mountain runs one of the country's oldest and most effective eating and exercise programs for women only. Those who come here know only too well that dieting does not work. In the hands of expert staff, women can steep themselves in the reality of their physiologies and take those first, very hard steps toward a new lifestyle of long-term weight management.

Resident dietitians and behavioral therapists teach their guests how to eat three balanced meals a day without abandoning the occasional sweet. Exercise physiologists help guests find an activity that they enjoy doing and design a fitness plan that they can realistically fit into their daily routine at home; choices include jogging, hiking, biking, cross-country skiing, belly dancing, and cardio-funk aerobics. Fitness plans start slowly, with gentle yet effective activities designed to help you experience bit by bit how good exercise can make you feel.

The atmosphere at Green Mountain is as well balanced as its methodology. There's some high-tech gym equipment here and swimming pools both indoors and out, but otherwise the grounds are generally clear of distractions. The simple setting encourages each woman to believe that she, and not the facilities of a spa resort, is key to achieving and maintaining her weight goals. Follow-up programs to help guests take this kind of thinking home include telephone counseling, newsletters, videos, audiocassettes, and special programs for repeat participants. A recent independent study published in the *International Journal of Eating Disorders* showed that 54 percent of Green Mountain "graduates" responding to the survey continued to lose weight or maintain weight loss five years after leaving the facility.

In its twenty-six years of working with dieting women, Green Mountain has gained a sensitivity for the emotional consequences of roller-coaster dieting. While optional massage sessions work wonders on the soul, it's the Body Image Therapy Program that directly addresses feelings of despair, anger, helplessness, and low self-esteem that can hinder weight management. Through a series of eight workshops over two weeks, participants in this program learn to shed their negative body image along with unwanted pounds. Special residency programs are also available for victims of dangerous fad diets — including, for example, Liquid Diet Recovery Program.

Retreats at Green Mountain require a serious commitment of time and energy. You have to get a medical checkup before going, and for lasting results, you should plan on a two- to four-week stay. It takes this long to gain the knowledge, coping skills, and positive attitude about eating and exercise that can keep the weight off for a lifetime.

**Season**   Open year-round; the peak season is from the end of May to the end of September. (Make reservations for these months far in advance, because enrollment is limited to forty-two guests at any one time.)

**Environs**   On twenty acres of private land in the Green Mountain National Forest of Vermont.

**Accommodations**   Standard and duplex rooms in a cozy converted ski lodge.

**Activities and Services**   Exercise and dance classes, jogging, hiking, biking. Tennis and cross-country skiing seasonally. Cooking and crafts classes, educational lectures, nutritional counseling, yoga. Private psychotherapy and massage for an additional fee.

**Religious Affiliation**   None.

**Rates**   One-week programs range from $825 to $1,850, two-week from $1,500 to $3,500, four-week from $2,800 to $6,000; the cost varies with season and room accommodations (the lowest rates are for triple accommodations during winter months, the highest for single rooms during summer months). Program fees include room, meals, seminars, fitness evaluations, select counseling sessions, and workshop materials.

**For More Information**   Green Mountain at Fox Run, Fox Lane, Box 164, Ludlow, Vt. 05149; phone (800) 448-8106 or (802) 228-8885; fax (802) 228-8887; Website: www.fitwoman.com.

---

## HEARTLAND SPA
## Gilman, Illinois

Located on thirty-two acres of prime Illinois farmland and boasting a private lake for water biking and swimming, this former dairy farm turned luxury spa offers its guests plenty of opportunities for pampering while also providing a glimpse into a new and healthier lifestyle. The spa could quite literally call itself a "wellness farm." Services make good use of the old dairy's outbuildings, and the former barn houses a state-of-the-art three-level gym and exercise facility.

Heartland's spa experience is a balanced program of sensible eating, good exercise, and a sound philosophy of stress management designed to relax and enrich even the most harried. Spa treatments offered include massage therapy, facials, manicures and pedicures, hair and skin care, and personal fitness assessments. The cuisine is classically low in fat and high in complex carbohydrates. As a bonus, the beautifully presented meals are made to be easily reproduced at home, encouraging guests to continue with what they have learned about good nutrition long after vacation is over.

**Season**   Year-round.

**Environs**   A lakefront mansion on a thirty-two-acre estate in Illinois farm country, just south of Chicago.

**Accommodations**   Double or single occupancy with private bath.

**Activities and Services**   Indoor swimming pool, saunas, steam room, whirlpools, tennis, outdoor track, exercise and aerobics studios, full treatment salon. Fishing, water biking, cross-country skiing and hiking trails, twenty-six exercise and relaxation classes.

**Religious Affiliation**   None.

**Rates**   Standard room rates are $378 (weekday), $420 (weekend). Seven-night stays range from $1,190 to $1,666 (with assigned roommate), or $2,380 to $2,646 (single occupancy).

**For More Information**   Heartland Spa, Kam Lake Estate, 1237 East 1600 North Road, Gilman, Ill. 60938; phone (800) 545-4853 or (815) 683-2182; fax (815) 683-2144; Website: www.heartlandspa.com.

---

Hollyhock
## Cortes Island, British Columbia, Canada

Hollyhock is a holistic community for experiential learning. Its alternative education programs are top rate, yet low keyed and low in cost. Located approximately one hundred miles north of Vancouver, it's accessible only by ferry or air. The remote setting affords guests a regenerative encounter with the natural world and with each other. You can choose from weekend getaways, weeklong holidays, or monthlong intensives; for those who wish to fully immerse themselves in the Hollyhock experience, there are opportunities for extended-stay work-study programs.

Hollyhock's offerings are vast, including more than seventy seminars and workshops. Subjects range from health, healing, and shamanism to t'ai chi and couples' retreats. Although the days are essentially unstructured, mornings begin with yoga and meditation; massage and bodywork are also available. There's a private lake and beaches for swimming and boating, and the guided nature walks are especially popular.

**Season**   Mid-March to September 1.

**Environs**   An island on the edge of the coastal wilderness of British Columbia.

**Accommodations**   Semiprivate and dormitory-style. Sites for camping are also available. Showers and sanitary facilities are located in heated buildings.

**Activities and Services**   Swimming (beaches, private lake), hot tub, nature walks, jogging, hiking, several kinds of boating. Massage, reflexology, acupressure, deep tissue massage, body wraps, facials.

**Religious Affiliation**   None.

**Rates**   Two-night packages vary from $119 (campsite) to $289 (single with shared bath); Seven-night packages from $309 (campsite) to $869 (single with shared bath). Three meals are included.

**For More Information**   Hollyhock, Box 127, Cortes Island, B.C. V0P1K0, Canada; phone (800) 933-6339; fax (250) 935-6424; Website: www.hollyhock.bc.ca.

---

## HOSTERIA LAS QUINTAS RESORT SPA
**Cuernavaca, Mexico**

This luxury spa offers spectacular and often mystical landscape scenery, lush body treatments, and great local Mexican and international cuisine all at an exchange rate favorable to those north of the border. What makes it unique among other Mexican and Caribbean spas, however, is that unlike destinations where foreigners gather as an island unto themselves, Hosteria Las Quintas finds inventive ways to bring its guests into contact with the variety and breadth of the Mexican landscape. A specialist in the eco-fitness tour, the spa's programs nicely blend exercise, culture, better health learning, and adventure.

The theory is this: Why go all the way to Mexico and step on a Stairmaster when you can run up the steps of an ancient Aztec pyramid? Why sit cross-legged staring at crystals where there are stalactite caves to explore as large as Carlsbad? Why lie in a chlorinated pool when you can float on a raft down miles of a crystal-clear river lined with royal palms and filled with brightly colored fish? For lovers of Mexican crafts, there is even an Aerobic Shopping Tour to the silver craftsmen's town of Taxco. Since vacations at this resort are unstructured and eco-fitness tours are offered daily, you can choose to participate in as many or as few of these health adventures as you desire. Opt out of the excursions and you can practice your custom-designed exercise routine (based on an initial medical and fitness evaluation at check-in) in the resort's modern gym or two heated pools. A full menu of spa services and beauty treatments is also offered à la carte or as part of a package.

**Season** Year-round.
**Environs** A walled estate property in the Mexican colonial city of Cuernavaca, about an hour and a half from Mexico City. The altitude is 4,703 feet.
**Accommodations** Classic Mexican-tiled interiors, simply decorated. All rooms have a terrace and some have a Jacuzzi or fireplace.
**Activities and Services** Hiking, horseback riding, river boating, pyramid climbing. Adventures to nearby volcanoes, the

lagoons of Zempoala, and Aztec ruins. A wide range of spa and beauty treatments including massage and shiatsu, reflexology, lymphatic drainage, cryotherapy, and body wraps and peels.

**Religious Affiliation**   None.

**Rates**   A seven-night eco-fitness program is U.S. $2,085 (single occupancy), or $1,745 (double); a four-night eco-fitness is $1,290 (single), or $1,096 (double). These rates include round-trip air transfers, room accommodations, all meals and nonalcoholic beverages, medical evaluation, fitness and body composition analysis, and redeemable points for spa or resort services, from facials to yoga and Spanish-language classes. Another bargain is the four-night Supreme Pampering Program for $1,146 (single occupancy), or $952 (double). Inquire about other packages.

**For More Information**   Hosteria Las Quintas, Boulevard Díaz Ordaz 9, Cuernavaca, Morelas, Mexico 62440; phone (5273) 18-3949; toll-free U.S. reservations (888) 772-7639; e-mail: hquintas@intersur.com.

---

## INDIAN OAK RESORT AND SPA
### Chesterton, Indiana

Indian Oak is a family-owned and -operated resort spa noted for its understated atmosphere and heartfelt commitment to the well-being of its guests. Approaching the resort grounds from the local road, you'll have to drive past two gas stations and a small strip mall. The resort's main buildings aren't very pretty from the outside, but inside you'll find some innovative spa services offered by a knowledgeable and sharing staff. The rooms are comfortable, with most offering views out onto a small lake surrounded by woods. These grounds located behind the building seem miles away from the high-traffic road and are laced with paths used for walking, jogging, or meditation.

The spa was founded in the early 1980s by Wingfield Chubb, who had holistic care in mind but in the end had to cater to a public somewhat skeptical of New Age techniques. Some idiosyncrasies survive from those days. The beauty salon still does a lot of hair and nails, and the resort's Irish pub is a popular local spot. But under the direction of Wingfield's daughter Cathy, Indian Oak is beginning to provide spa services that fully realize her father's plans. She has hired new staff and even flown in a chef from New York to create the pub's tasty vegan menu.

Spa services can rival those of premier destinations. They include La Stone therapy massage, seaweed rejuvenating facials, aromatherapy, and Ayurvedic treatments. Well-Life Workshops in yoga, relaxation, and qi gong are also run from the spa. You'll want to arrange for a spa package (treatments are usually à la carte). Worth mentioning is a two-and-a-half-hour aromatic Tranquility Experience designed to bring you bliss from the inside out. It begins in a massage chair leaning over fragrant steam to cleanse the sinuses, then moves on to a hydrotherapy table for an all-over sea salt scrub followed by a Vichy shower. Next, in a room with dim lights and soft music, comes a light oleation massage and an all-over steam treatment (at the peak of which an ice pack is placed on your heart). At last follows shirodhara, the gentle flow of oils onto the center of your forehead (the place of our Third Eye, or spiritual eye).

While spa services are available daily, fitness and yoga classes are generally held once per week (without charge). One-on-one instruction in t'ai chi, yoga, and meditation can be arranged on request, or talk to the resort staff about gathering some friends or family for a group retreat. Personal growth workshops are scheduled on special weekends, and can include Fine Tune Your Intuition, Opening Your Heart to Angels, or Touching Your Life Purpose Work. An annual Relaxation Festival in early February attracts some noteworthy visiting faculty for three days of workshops, lectures, and fitness classes.

**Season**   Year-round.

**Environs**   In the heart of Indiana Dunes country, between Illinois and Michigan, only one hour from South Bend or Chicago. Free shuttle service to and from Porter County Regional Airport and the Dune Park train station is provided.

**Accommodations**   Lakeside or woodside rooms with private balcony and patio, and your choice of double or king-size beds. There is a cozy fireplace room and relaxing whirlpool room for special stays.

**Activities and Services**   Full-service spa and salon (massages, facials, herbal wraps, manicures, and more). Hiking trails, some boating and fishing, indoor pool for swimming and water exercise classes, step aerobics, qi gong, and relaxation meditation. Gym (Stairmasters, treadmills, and Universal weights), sauna, steam room, and whirlpool.

**Religious Affiliation**   None.

**Rates**   Rooms from $80 to $160, some with fireplace or whirlpool. Call for special weekend rates. Spa packages include two meals only; room rates include continental breakfast.

**For More Information**   Indian Oak, 528 Indian Boundary Road, Chesterton, Ind. 46304; phone (800) 552-4232 or (219) 926-2200; Website: www.indianoak.com.

## KENWOOD INN AND SPA
### Kenwood, California

This twelve-suite inn and spa in northern California's Sonoma Valley, set on a hillside overlooking a thousand acres of estate vineyards, appears on the horizon like a scene from Tuscany. Inside its walls, carefully chosen antiques accentuate Kenwood's feel of an Italian country villa. A sanctuary of Old World charm, Kenwood is loved for its comforts as well as its grace. Spa programs for relaxation and beauty pamper the body and soul. Choices include full-body massage, aromatherapy body polishes, and oxygen and vitamin A facials. While this all makes for a splendid respite from the modern world, it's another spa service that tells how a vacation here can be transformative as well as indulgent. The Ti Amo Togetherness Massage, a spa service for couples, is exemplary of how Kenwood caters to romance. Whether through the shared experience of therapeutic touch or quiet walks through grounds straight out of a costume drama, Kenwood is a place to get back in touch with the person who complements you. No exotic metaphysics, no strenuous talk or behavioral science, just a simple opportunity for people to restore intimacy and balance in their emotional lives.

**Season**  Year-round.
**Environs**  Four European-style country villas on secluded acres of vineyards and sloping hills located in Sonoma Valley, in the heart of northern California's wine country.
**Accommodations**  Luxury rooms (each decorated differently) with courtyard or countryside views. First-class cuisine and special-request breakfasts.

**Activities and Services**   A luxury retreat for rest and relaxation with a wide range of therapeutic massages, facials, and body treatments. Swimming, hiking, and cycling are popular.
**Religious Affiliation**   None.
**Rates**   Doubles range from $285 to $395 in the high season (April to the end of October), $255 to $365 in low season (November to the end of March).
**For More Information**   Kenwood Inn and Spa, 1400 Sonoma Highway, Kenwood, Calif. 95452; phone (800) 353-6966; Website: www.kenwoodinn.com

---

## KUSHI INSTITUTE
### Becket, Massachusetts

Michio and Aveline Kushi founded this institute in 1978 to teach others the commonsense lifestyle of a macrobiotic diet. For more than twenty years since then, the Kushi Institute has attracted visitors from around the world to its informative classes. Beginners to macrobiotics, and even to cooking, are welcome. So, too, are experienced cooks. Indeed, the Kushi Institute provides career training programs in macrobiotic cookery. The Ritz Carlton Hotel Company among others, has sent its chefs here to learn to create healthful yet tasty menu choices. Other participants arrive with specific health concerns such as hypertension, high or low blood sugar, ulcers, obesity, and even cancer, looking to use the natural, macrobiotic approach to health recovery. Such guests should schedule private counseling sessions to fine-tune dietary and lifestyle practices to their conditions.

A macrobiotic diet is not only health conscious but ecologically sound, with meals prepared from fresh, all-natural ingredients consisting mostly of whole grains, beans, vegetables, sea vegetables (yes, that means seaweed), and fruits. Kushi teaches its guests to choose the right foods, explaining why others are not recommended and what effects food can produce on your body, mind, and spirit. Some classes are cooking demonstrations; others are hands-on. Other types of practical instruction include tips on how to eat while traveling, how to prepare natural home remedies for relief from conditions such as fatigue, hypoglycemia, aches and pains, digestive disorders, and stress, and (most fun of all) how to give a tension-relieving shiatsu massage for the neck and shoulders. Because support is so important in maintaining a macrobiotic lifestyle, participants are encouraged to attend the seminar with a family member or friend.

A sample day in Kushi's seven-day Way to Health Program starts at 7 A.M. with gentle stretching exercises and a light breakfast, followed by an hour of free time. The day's cooking class begins at 10 A.M. Lunch, logically, follows. A long afternoon lecture (about two and a half hours) and another evening lecture (about two hours) are slotted between periods of scheduled free time and dinner. Recreational activities are up to you; nothing is organized. Walk, rest, or read, but don't expect to hit the Berkshire antiques shops, ski slopes, or nearby Tanglewood outdoor concerts, since no one slot of free time is long enough for extended excursions.

Another, less intensive offering is called Relax and Renew. In this more flexible program, you can choose your own dates and length of stay and use the Kushi Institute's healthful, country-manor style environment as a door to experience the New England scenery and attractions. As for educational activities, you have your choice of sitting in on as many or as few classes as you like during the length of your stay. Optimally, your stay should coincide with a Way to Health Program.

**Season**   Year-round.

**Environs**   Located in the heart of the Berkshire Mountains, set amid six hundred acres of secluded meadows, woodlands, and streams. Kushi is a ninety-minute drive from the Albany (New York) and Hartford (Connecticut) airports, and twenty minutes from Lee, Massachusetts.

**Accommodations**   Shared double rooms with shared baths. A limited number of private rooms, some with baths, available at higher cost.

**Activities and Services**   Macrobiotic cooking classes and lectures, gentle exercise and hiking paths.

**Religious Affiliation**   None.

**Rates**   Way to Health Program: one participant $1,495; two or more $1,395; pay thirty days in advance and save $100 off program fees. The Women's Wellness Weekend costs less than $500. Other types of stay at the Kushi Institute can range from $75 to 125 per night per person, including meals and selected activities. A private macrobiotic counseling session with a Kushi Institute senior teacher is $225.

**For More Information**   Kushi Institute, Box 7, Becket, Mass. 01223; phone (800) 975-8744 or (413) 623-5741; e-mail: kushi@macrobiotics.org.

------

## LA CASA DE VIDA NATURAL
**Luquillo, Puerto Rico**

This unique and exceedingly intimate retreat sits on a foothill of El Yunque, the national rain forest park named for the Taíno Indian god of happiness. Commanding a view of the ocean and within an easy drive of five beaches, La Casa de Vida Natural offers five-day workshops in natural living for only eight guests at a time.

Fitness here is combined with outdoor adventure. Mountain trails take the place of step machines, guests float in oceans rather than flotation tanks, and Jacuzzis are forsaken in favor of a nearby sparkling mountain waterfall. Even the spa treatments are drawn from the environment: Mud for facials is dug from El Yunque, seaweed for body wraps is harvested at a local remote beach, and herbs are gathered on the resort grounds only minutes before their use.

Generally, three classes are offered per day, including meditation and movement and introductory intensives in vegetarian food preparation and detoxification. Lolling on a beach is always an option, while some prefer more aerobic excursions such as hiking, snorkeling, and kayaking. No activity is required. All participants are free to choose whatever sport, eco-adventure, or treatment they feel is appropriate to their own needs and interests.

A bargain of a spa, especially for so privy a retreat; some say the only thing that can account for this ideal Caribbean health adventure is magical realism. Others thank the Taíno god of happiness the next hill over.

**Season** Year-round, but be advised that September is peak hurricane season.
**Environs** A remote Caribbean island retreat in the foothills of a national rainforest park, with the ocean in view. It's near mountain streams, cascades, thermal waters, and hidden beaches; about an hour from the airport at San Juan.
**Accommodations** Modest rooms in the main house (a renovated farmhouse) or guest cottages, some with private bath. Vegetarian meals with surprising flavor.
**Activities and Services** Hidden-beach and kayak excursions, guided rain forest hikes, boating, snorkeling in the ocean and mountain streams, aerobics. Movement and t'ai chi classes.

Massage, acupuncture, polarity therapy, thalassotherapy, mud baths, and various body rubs, glows, and wraps.

**Religious Affiliation**   None.

**Rates**   Workshops range, depending mostly on season, from $595 to $825 (single accommodations), or $535 to $750 (double). Private rooms are $150 extra. Cost includes lodging, three meals daily, yoga and meditation, beach transfers, all excursions, and select spa treatments.

**For More Information**   La Casa de Vida Natural, Box 1919, Río Grande, Luquillo, P.R. 00745; phone (809) 887-4359 or (212) 260-5823 (New York reservations offices).

---

## LAKE AUSTIN SPA RESORT
### Austin, Texas

At Lake Austin, guests can discover their own sense of balance between periods of relaxation and exercise. The spa offers twelve daily fitness and body-strengthening classes, myriad outdoor activities including guided hikes and canoe trips, and ample time for its guests to meditate or simply unwind while strolling or bird-watching along the shores of its scenic lake. Fitness trainers encourage progress with good sense but, in this laid-back atmosphere, they generally respond rather than lecture to guests seeking knowledge of a healthy and active lifestyle. Spa technicians, on the other hand, attract greater notice with their luxury care. For exquisite pampering, try the seven-night Ultimate Pampering Package, which includes luxury accommodations, spa cuisine three times daily, and treatment after treatment (fourteen in all) of massage, bodywork, cleansing facials, gentle eye lifts, and facial peels.

**Season**   Year-round.

**Environs**   A lakeside retreat in the heart of the East Texas hill country.

**Accommodations**   Garden apartments and cottages, all with lake views. There's a roommate-matching service for single guests.

**Activities and Services**   Hiking, tennis, water sports, sculling, water biking, canoeing, kayaking, walking. Twenty-four-hour training room with complete facilities, sauna, steam room, Jacuzzi. Cooking classes, organic gardening, yoga, personal training sessions, spa treatments.

**Religious Affiliation**   None.

**Rates**   All rates include meals and services. Nightly rates begin at $280 (per person, single occupancy). A three-night Refresher Package (private) is $1,090, four-night $1,290, seven-night $1,990. Also, the seven-night Living Well Program is $2,290.

**For More Information**   Lake Austin Spa Resort, 1705 Quinlan Park Road, Austin, Tex. 78732; phone (512) 266-2444; Website: www.lakeaustin.com.

---

## MIRAVAL, LIFE IN BALANCE
## Catalina, Arizona

Life in Balance means precisely that. At Miraval the food is healthful yet gourmet, the scene elegant, and the services attentive without the feeling of escapist resort indulgence. Emphasis here is placed squarely on stress reduction, self-discovery, mind-body interaction, and the pleasure of the vacationers. No one is made to feel starved or overexerted. Spa services can be indulgent, but largely remain focused on healing and relaxation rather than beauty.

Miraval has no fixed curriculum, offering instead a dizzying array of recreational activities and life-enhancing programs.

(Remember that some programs fill up, while others require advance sign-up on a sheet near the lobby.) For guests troubled over what to do first—or worse, who suffer from the self-defeating habit of trying to do it all—resort guides can recommend confidence courses in Voice Expression or, more directly, Mindful Decision Making. Other mind-body management options include an equine workshop, meditation, mind-body dance, t'ai chi, yoga, role playing, art and music courses, and massage workshops.

The equine workshops deserve special mention. Once upon a time, Miraval's campus was the home of an addiction recovery clinic; a basic workshop with horses was designed by its resident therapist and a recovering addict to foster self-awareness. As those familiar with riding know, body language speaks so loud and clear to a horse when you're trying to control its movements that on horseback, you have no alternative but to address outward expressions of festering insecurity, anger, reluctance, or fear.

Fitness enthusiasts will enjoy Miraval's challenging Quantum Leap Program or the chance to climb a thirty-two-foot rock wall, while relaxation groupies can dig ample opportunities for meditation, yoga, walks in Zen desert gardens, and New Age spa therapies. The menu of spa treatments here is twelve pages long, with choices that can make shiatsu sound like a real bore. Since Tucson is where hot-stone therapy got its start, you won't want to miss out on Miraval's trademark version, in which smooth basalt rocks are heated to 140 degrees in water than pulled out with tongs, placed under your back, and used to massage every last knot out of your arms, legs, fingers, and toes. For a cool-down, try a dip in the trilevel outdoor pool, or lie poolside where hidden mist jets refresh you from the desert heat.

**Season**   Year-round. The peak season is October to May; the off-peak is June to September.

**Environs**   Adobe buildings appear as one with the desert landscape and rising Santa Catalina Mountains. The spa is about forty-five minutes from Tucson International Airport.

**Accommodations**   Elegant casita-style rooms and suites clustered in five Mexican-style villages; all rooms feature twice-daily maid service.

**Activities and Services**   Aerobics, yoga, t'ai chi, meditation, mind-body dance, weight and cardiovascular training, fitness profiles, cooking demonstrations. Hiking, rock climbing on a faux monolith, horseback riding, golf, bicycling, volleyball, croquet, four swimming pools, and two tennis courts. Myriad body and skin treatments, massages, and other relaxation treatments and salon services. Art and music courses are also available.

**Religious Affiliation**   None.

**Rates**   Spa packages off season range from $220 to $700

(double accommodations), or $300 to $900 (single, per person per night). In-season rates are from $375 to $850 (double accommodations), or $475 to $1,050 (single, per person per night). Costs include lodging, all meals and nonalcoholic beverages, all group activities, choice of one personal service or consultation (a massage, perhaps, or a facial or tennis lesson) and round-trip Tucson Airport transfers.

**For More Information** Miraval, Life in Balance, 5000 East Via Estancia Miraval, Catalina, Ariz. 85739; phone (800) 232-3969 or (520) 825-4000; fax (520) 825-5163; e-mail: miravalaz@aol.com; Website: www.miravalresort.com.

---

## FOR MORE HORSING AROUND . . .

*Hills Health and Guest Ranch, British Columbia* This resort spa offers six-night vacations of western fun under the Cinemascopic sky of the Canadian outback. Enjoy horseback riding, singalong hayrides, and campfires at Willy's Wigwam. If bouncing around in wagons makes you sore, the Hills is also home to the Canadian Wellness Center. Combining treatments with adult education, the center offers bodywork and beauty services along with fitness activities, nutritional planning, and health lectures. Guests can also enjoy all of the above while participating in a supervised ten-night weight-loss program. *Rooms:* Single, double, or triple accommodations in two main lodges or woodsy A-frame chalets. *Rates:* Wilderness Adventures from $1,412; Stress Management Vacations from $1,384; Weight Loss (ten nights) from $1,756; meals and fitness assessment are included. *For More Information:* Hills Health Ranch, C-26, 108 Mile Road, B.C. V0K 270, Canada; phone (250) 791-5225; fax (250) 791-6384.

## NEW AGE HEALTH SPA
### Neversink, New York

New Age Health Spa is not what it sounds. Sure, you can schedule astrological or tarot consultations here, but the real focus is on holistic health. Guests spend about five hours a day exercising, with another two dedicated to meditation and gentle movement classes such as t'ai chi or yoga. Lectures and evening programs are offered, but optional. Many prefer to curl up with a book or head straight to sleep, especially after their first day of waking at 6 A.M.

Days begin with early-morning Zen meditation, an aerobic walk and yoga, followed by breakfast and a nutrition seminar. Fitness classes happen from late morning to late afternoon, with breaks for lunch and a one-hour fitness seminar. The wind-down starts at 4 P.M. with yoga or t'ai chi, followed by guided meditation, dinner, an evening program, and a movie. Join in on all activities or only some. Meals are provided, emphasizing complex carbohydrates with moderate protein and low fat. Individuals with special diet needs are cheerfully accommodated.

No minimum stay is required here, and activities are not incremental in scope, so guests can count on each day offering equal possibilities. The spa's motto is Challenge by Choice, which means that everyone sets their own pace and goals — but they work toward these goals in the company of others. A good example of how guests can work as a team while exploring their own limits is the High Ropes Course and Alpine Tower. Deceptively simple in appearance, this fifty-foot vertical structure is a complex network of ropes, pullies, and levers posing a challenge that requires strategy, stamina, and strength to climb.

For a more structured program limited to twelve participants, New Age offers a six-day/five-night Lifestyles Program.
And don't forget about spa treatments. After all, a goal of balanced living can't be met without a few indulgences now and
then.

**Season**    Year-round. The peak season and times include July,
August, and all weekends and holidays during other months.

**Environs**    White houses with French windows on 165 rolling
acres of countryside in the Catskills of New York, about two
and a half hours from New York City.

**Accommodations**    Country-inn-style rooms. Your choice of
single, double, or triple accommodations (roommates are
matched up on request).

**Activities and Services**    Fitness and aerobic classes, stretching and toning, Zen and guided meditation, yoga, t'ai chi, kick
boxing. New 420-foot solarium with indoor pool, whirlpool,
steam room, sauna, weight and exercise rooms. Private fitness,
nutritional, hypnotherapy, astrological, and tarot consultations
available. Spa services include a wide range of facials
(Ayurvedic, European, paraffin, and OJA), body therapies
(aromatherapy, reflexology, shiatsu), and body treatments
(Ayurvedic detox, full-body rejuvenation, milk and honey,
expectant mother treatment, Moor mud).

**Religious Affiliation**    None.

**Rates**    Program fees—including accommodations, all meals
and snacks, and use of facilities—range from $737 weekly,
$114 daily (triple standard), to $1,224 weekly, $193 daily
(single standard). The Lifestyles Program fee is $2,250. Add
$20 per day per person for all stays during peak season and
times. Spa services are available à la carte.

**For More Information**    New Age Health Spa, Neversink,
N.Y. 12765; phone (800) 682-4348 or (914) 985-7600; fax

(914) 985-2467. E-mail newagespa@zelacom.com; Website
www.newagehealthspa.com.

―――――――――

## OMEGA INSTITUTE FOR HOLISTIC STUDIES
### Rhinebeck, New York

Omega Institute may offer spa treatments, but it is no spa.
Omega is better described as a spiritual summer camp for
adults. Nearly twelve thousand visitors per year flock to this
lakeside oasis in the Hudson River Valley to attend a total of
250 workshops and programs given by a veritable Who's Who
of New Age thinkers. Faculty members range from medical
doctors to best-selling authors, musicians, and dancers as well
as religious leaders.

Those unfamiliar with the types of workshops offered at
Omega may want to consider attending a special introductory
weekend. This package features an introduction to yoga, meditation, t'ai chi, and movement and offers workshops in self-
discovery, body awareness, stress reduction, spirituality, and
wellness.

The source of Omega's rise to fame, however, is its Wellness Program. Offered four times per year (three beginner
weeks and one advanced weekend) and coordinated by
Stephen Rechtschaffen, M.D., this vacation offers core programs in the principles and practices of holistic health, fitness
and exercise, and Timeshifting—an innovative and very popular stress-reduction method developed at the University of
Massachusetts.

When not attending workshops or gabbing at the campus
café, Omega guests enjoy access to more typical resort activities: tennis, basketball, swimming and boating on the lake, and
evening concerts and dances.

**Season**   Year-round.

**Environs**   The Hudson River Valley of New York, approximately two hours north of Manhattan and about three hours from Boston.

**Accommodations**   Double rooms, most in cottages with private or shared baths (roommates are assigned if you come alone). Other options include dormitory housing (eight small partitioned rooms with shared bathrooms) or camping facilities. Single rooms with private or shared baths are available, but limited in number. Meals are included in accommodations fees.

**Activities and Services**   Courses and workshops on health, personal development, creativity, spirituality, stress reduction. Tennis, basketball, swimming, boating. Holistic therapies, nutritional counseling, massage, facials, sauna available for reasonable fees.

**For More Information**   Omega Institute, 260 Lake Drive, Rhinebeck, N.Y. 12572-3212; (800) 944-1001; Website: www.omega-inst.org.

---

## PRITIKIN LONGEVITY CENTERS
### Miami, Florida, and Santa Monica, California

Pritikin Longevity Centers are prototype medspas: They combine the healing experience of a spa vacation with a crash course on the ins and outs of preventative medicine. Their aim is to bring about physical changes in how—and for how long—you live your life. These are not places to visit on a whim. Their programs require a serious health commitment and a minimum one-week stay.

The Pritikin approach to longevity has remained virtually unchanged as diet trends have come and gone, and while science has contradicted its research findings from one year to the next. One reason for this consistency is that the Pritikin diet and lifestyle plays it safe. Guidelines are difficult to follow, but as one nutritionist at the Florida center vows, "I lost most of my family to heart disease and no matter what the future of medicine unfolds, I fervently believe that following Pritikin standards will have saved my life."

Those standards outline which foods to eat, as well as how much, how often, and at what time of the day. Six light meals per day are recommended over the all-too-common habit of skipping breakfast, lunch, or both, and overcompensating for hunger at night. The last of these six meals is finished before 7 P.M. Diet restrictions include never eating sugar or flour products, such as bread, cookies, cake, and pretzels. Butters and margarine are also taboo, as are chocolate and coffee (not even decaf is allowed).

If the Pritikin approach sounds meaningful to your life but the diet a little hard to digest, a visit to one of the Pritikin Centers can help you fully appreciate the reasons behind their lifestyle approach. Following their guidelines out of a textbook is helpful, but it's not likely to firm your resolve as significantly. Those who do come do so for many reasons: to lose weight, stop smoking, lower their blood pressure, prevent the use of insulin in diabetes that begins after middle age, or simply cope better in life through diet and exercise. Most are over forty. Some bring loved ones so that they might gain sensitivity for their new eating habits and lifestyle changes. All guests leave with an individualized fitness regime designed to suit their daily routine and interests.

Lectures make up a large part of your time at Pritikin. Other health-minded destinations, because they are resorts foremost, try to give a casual, living-room atmosphere to their lectures. At Pritikin, education is serious and straightforward. Lecturers get out the slide projectors, microphones, and chalkboard pointers without worrying about looking like your last, seemingly unapproachable college professor. They can do this because Pritikin guests know what they're there for, and that's information on extending their lives.

Cooking classes are demonstrations (not hands-on)—which may be disappointing for some, but it generally allows for more instruction in a limited amount of time. If it's individual attention you're hoping for, don't be surprised if the chef hands out his e-mail address and offers to wire you weekly health tips. Other methods of support anticipate the hour guests leave the center to go it on their own. The best of these is a planned shopping excursion, during which Pritikin staff will go with you to the grocery store and guide you through a typical week's selection of foods.

Another integral part of Pritikin lifestyle education is coping exercises, ranging from a helpful, humorous mantra (several former guests have these sayings on T-shirts) and simple relaxation skills to acute stress-management training. Therapeutic massage and hypnotherapy are available in Florida for a fee, with the California center offering even more relaxing amenities. If that's not enough to set your mind at ease, you'll be glad to know that after you leave Pritikin, your program coordinator is only a phone call away.

**Season**   Year-round.

**Environs**   Santa Monica center occupies an entire beachfront hotel. The Miami center is also located beachfront, but inside the 1940s and somewhat nostalgic Flamingo Hotel building. Plans are currently under way for the Florida center to move to a new, more modern facility with more room to offer program amenities.

**Accommodations**   Rooms vary from standard to luxe. All have private bath and your choice of single or double accommodations.

**Activities and Services**   Medical, fitness, and nutritional counseling, cooking demonstrations, group exercise, relaxation classes, massage, other spa and beauty services.

**Religious Affiliation**   None.

**Rates**   The standard one-week program fee is $3,305 for the principal participant and $1,555 for a companion participant; two-week $6,085 principal, $2,475 companion; three- and four-week programs are also available. Meals are included, but lodging is in addition to the program fee and can range from $85 to $850 for one week, $130 to $1,250 for two weeks, depending on room type and occupancy. Medical examinations are extra; some medical service fees may be covered under your individual health-insurance policy terms and diagnosis, but even in these instances, you (and not the Pritikin Center) must be reimbursed.

**For More Information**   In Florida: Pritikin Longevity Center, 5875 Collins Avenue, Miami, Fla. 33140; phone (800) 327-4914; fax (305) 866-1872; e-mail: pritikinfl@aol.com. In California: 1910 Ocean Front Walk, Santa Monica, Calif. 90405; phone (800) 421-9911 or (310) 450-5433; fax (310) 829-6229; e-mail: pritikinca@aol.com.

---

RED MOUNTAIN
**(Formerly Franklin Quest Institute of Fitness)**
**Ivins, Utah**

Many resorts and spas promise spectacular scenery in brochure after brochure. But make no mistake, Red Mountain delivers stunning sunrises and sweeping landscape vistas day in and out. Named for the surrounding red canyon walls, this fitness spa is within a short distance of Zion, Bryce Canyon, and Capitol Reef National Parks. The hiking trails guests make most use of are in Snow Canyon State Park.

Red Mountain vacations focus on good health and weight maintenance through a combination of exercise, time and stress management, and mastering nutritional skills. Weight loss is often a part of this experience, but Red Mountain insists that true health and well-being come from achieving goals and not from reading the scale. The belief is that reaching high, yet realistic goals can leave guests feeling empowered and in control of their lives.

Although the spa houses a complete fitness center, hiking and walking form the primary focus of exercise and fitness training. One advantage of this is the chance to view the natural scenery; another is that by hitting the trail instead of the Stairmaster, participants learn that they don't need a high-tech gym or fitness trainer to continue their exercise routines at home. Outdoor tours for all levels of difficulty are available; guests strap on their hiking boots to the mantra, Get Out and Move.

In terms of nutrition, Red Mountain teaches that there are natural laws that govern total mental and body health. If obeyed, these laws result in disease prevention, weight loss, proper management of time and stress, and a sense of wellness that promotes confidence and realizes potential in every aspect of life.

**Season**   Year-round. The high season is September to November and March to May.

**Environs**   The red rock country of southern Utah, near eight national and state parks.

**Accommodations**   Quads (four beds), doubles (two beds), private (one bed).

**Activities and Services**  Walking, hiking (all levels), biking and mountain biking, fitness and weight training, spinning, swimming, hot tub, tennis, studio and water aerobics, yoga, t'ai chi. Spa treatments include massage (Swedish, deep tissue, aromatherapy, Russian), loofah treatments, aloe aroma wraps, body glows, hydrating and deep cleansing treatments, and foot, hair, and nail care.

**Religious Affiliation**  None.

**Rates**  From $735 to $1,590 single, per week, depending on level of accommodations and season. Fees include lodging, meals, all lectures and demos, fitness classes, and full use of spa facilities. Spa treatments are à la carte, but discount packages are available. For participants with budget concerns, a special rate of $615 a week applies to those staying in town at the lodging of their choice.

**For More Information**  Red Mountain, 202 North Snow Canyon Road, Ivins, Utah 84738; phone (800) 407-3002; fax (435) 652-5755; Website: www.redmountainspa.com.

---

## ROWE CAMP AND CONFERENCE CENTER
**Rowe, Massachusetts**

Rowe Camp operates as an adult summer camp and learning center. Founded in 1924, its mission is to provide an atmosphere in which people can make better sense of their lives and become inspired to affect the world in which they live in a positive way. The principles are Unitarian Universalist, but all spiritual paths are respected and even encouraged. First and foremost, Rowe Camp focuses on community and acceptance. This is a place to find your vocation, improve relationships, see the world from a new perspective, or simply get back to the basics of fun.

Workshops are small, intimate forums taught by instructors outstanding in their fields (some are world renowned, while others are deeply committed teachers known for their work on a smaller scale). A staple offering of Rowe Camp is Kindred Spirits. Now ten years old, this is a weeklong program of positive, uplifting, fun-filled growth-producing experiences. Another favorite is Women Circles, a program for exploring, redefining, and celebrating womanhood, currently in its twenty-third year. Other workshops deal with specific topics in the areas of creativity, self-expression, relationships, spiritual exploration, and body awareness and acceptance.

**Season**    In full operation during the summer; fall, winter, and spring months offer weekend retreats only.

**Environs**    Rowe's buildings are folded into the slope of gentle mountains at the edge of an old New England village in the Berkshires of western Massachusetts. The camp is forty minutes from either Williamstown or Greenfield.

**Accommodations**    Dorm-style housing (with single and bunk beds) in winterized cabins, summer camp cabins, and a farmhouse; the all-season bathhouse is in a separate building from the cabins. Bring your own toiletries, towels, and bedding, and be sure to specify any preference for male, female, or coed housing. A limited number of single- and double-occupancy private rooms located in the farmhouse are available on a first-come, first-served basis; campers are also welcome (bring your own tent), or you can lodge in a nearby inn, bed-and-breakfast, or motel.

**Activities and Services**    Workshops vary each season. Camp fun activities include walks in the woods, swimming, canoeing, storytelling and singing around a campfire, dancing, dialogue, and, yes, a guest talent show. Ski areas are located within twenty-five miles, including Mount Snow.

**Religious Affiliation** Rowe Camp is a nonprofit organization affiliated with the Unitarian Universalist Church, but receives no financial support from it. Nor does Rowe proselytize.

**Rates** Sliding-scale program fees range from $150 to $230 (based on gross income). Separate fees for meals and housing range from $90 to $165. Work study is possible; call for an application.

**For More Information** Rowe Camp and Conference Center, King's Highway Road, Rowe, Mass. 01367; phone (413) 339-4954; fax (413) 339-5728; e-mail: retreat@rowecenter.org; Website: www.RoweCenter.org.

---

## SONOMA MISSION INN AND SPA
### Boyes Hot Springs, California

The Sonoma Mission Inn, with its trademark pink stucco hotel, has been the toast of northern Californians since the early 1900s. In the beginning, guests came to soak their toxins away in the artesian mineral pools. While the springs are still popular (a new one was tapped in 1991), the Mission Inn has since grown into a veritable palace of earthly pleasures. Pampering abounds, but guests also come for the fitness training. The high-tech exercise facilities and around-the-clock fitness classes will not disappoint guests seeking a vigorous workout. Enologists, however, may prefer to go outside on a hike or bicycle tour of wine country.

**Season** Year-round.

**Environs** A luxurious-wine country resort surrounded by eight acres of eucalyptus-shaded grounds; it's forty-five minutes north of San Francisco.

**Accommodations**  Standard and garden rooms in the main building, with full (and very attentive) hotel services. Some theme rooms are available.

**Activities and Services**  Complete line of exercise equipment in the fitness pavilion, including free weights and a wide variety of exercise machines. Also aerobics, yoga, Jacuzzi, sauna, steam room, swimming. Spa treatments include hot artesian mineral springs, facials, meditation, mud and clay baths, body packs and scrubs, shiatsu, massage, aromatherapy, image and nutritional counseling.

**Religious Affiliation**  None.

**Rates**  High-season rooms range from $185 to $750, low-season $155 to $595. Seasonal spa packages are $170 to $350 (per person, double occupancy).

**For More Information**  Sonoma Mission Inn and Spa, 18140 Sonoma Highway 12, Boyes Hot Springs, Calif. 95476; phone (800) 862-4945 or (707) 938-9000; fax (707) 996-5358; e-mail: smi@smispa.com; Website: www.sonomamissioninn.com.

---

STRUCTURE HOUSE
**Durham, North Carolina**

Structure House provides exactly what its name implies—a highly structured and supervised environment specializing in weight loss, weight control, and weight maintenance for people with chronic and long-term weight problems. To ensure lasting results, Structure House also provides educational opportunities that help guests grasp more fully the psychological and physical issues inherent in the problems they face.

Newcomers are advised to stay for at least one month (although shorter sessions and programs are available). It often takes this long for guests to seriously begin changing their lifelong patterns of behavior. Staff members are watchful and firm but caring, encouraging guests to set their own long- and short-term goals. Physical, medical, and psychological counseling as well as nutritional instruction and diet planning are all a part of the plan. Guests leave Structure House with new knowledge and skills, and with the option to maintain contact with the staff. Some will go it alone; others choose to return on a regular basis to chart their progress and reaffirm their commitment.

At first blush, Structure House may seem an expensive solution to a very old problem. However, for those with chronic weight problems who are exasperated by endless rounds of fad diets, the results are indeed life changing and well worth the price.

**Season** Year-round.

**Environs** Durham is a large southern college town with much to offer.

**Accommodations** One- and two-bedroom private apartments with weekly maid service.

**Activities and Services** Aerobics, golf, tennis, horseback riding, full line of fitness equipment, indoor and outdoor pools, massage. Also, health counseling.

**Religious Affiliation** None.

**Rates** The eight-night full program (single) of $7,196 includes all meals, physical assessment, psychological treatment, health education, medical evaluation of current health problems, and monitoring for health maintenance.

**For More Information** Structure House, 3017 Pickett Road, Durham, N.C. 27705; phone (800) 553-0052 or (919) 493-4205; fax (919) 490-0191; e-mail: info@structurehouse.com; Website: www.structurehouse.com.

## AND FOR MORE INCHES OFF . . .

*Duke University Diet and Fitness Center*    Durham is also home
to another celebrated place for weight management. For
almost thirty years, Duke University has offered its state-
of-the-art facilities and highly professional staff to members
of the public suffering from conditions of chronic overweight. The goal here is changing not diet, but lifestyle.
Guests have intensive interaction with the staff, and are
encouraged to bring along a friend or relative to ensure that
they will be fully supported by loved ones who understand
the nature of their work. Results can be significant; studies
have shown that 70 percent of participants maintained or
exceeded their weight goal for at least one year after their
visit. *Rooms and Rates:* Program fees average $5,595 per
person, per week, accommodations not included. Off-site
lodging is available from $59 per night in nearby Duke
Tower, or in rooms in private homes averaging $100 per
week. *For More Information:* Duke University Diet and Fitness Center, 304 Trinity Avenue, Durham, N.C. 27701;
phone (800) 362-8446 or (919) 684-6631; fax (919) 682-
8869; Website: dmi-www.mc.duke.edu/dfc/home.html.

## TENNESSEE FITNESS SPA
## Waynesboro, Tennessee

People come to this spa in the Blue Ridge Mountains to lose
weight through exercise. Programs are structured, with guests'
activities organized from Sunday to Sunday. Private trainers
are available, but most guests prefer to stay within their

assigned groups. Groups are small, since total enrollment is limited to sixty-seven guests per week.

The average day begins with breakfast and a morning walk, which can be as short as two miles or as long as twelve, depending on the individual's ability and fitness. For nature lovers, longer is better. The surrounding landscape is a natural curiosity—the only double-span natural bridge formation in the world. There is also a cave spouting steam and a crystal-clear creek bordering the resort grounds.

After this healthy morning start, the rest of the day can be spent on aerobics, "swimnastics," step classes, weight training, and stretching. Nutrition and fitness lectures are held in the afternoon, while evenings offer more recreational activities such as volleyball, pool games, and cooking classes.

**Season** Late February to early December.
**Environs** Scenic forested land in Tennessee's Natural Bridge country, only ninety-five miles southwest of Nashville.
**Accommodations** A wide choice of room accommodations is available, from the budget-minded ladies' quad (four twin beds with two baths) to the privacy and indulgence of a lake-view lodge or penthouse suite. Some off-campus housing and motor homes are available at a lesser cost.
**Activities and Services** Exercise classes, swimming, hiking; golf, tennis, canoeing, horseback riding nearby. Massages, facials, manicures, personal fitness training available at an added cost.
**Religious Affiliation** None.
**Rates** Prices range from $550 to $2,400 per person per week, depending on room type, occupancy, and season of stay; this includes all meals, snacks, beverages, lodging with daily maid service, lectures and classes, and free use of all facilities.

**For More Information**    Tennessee Fitness Spa, 299 Natural Bridge Park Road, Waynesboro, Tenn. 38485; phone (931) 722-5589; Website: www.TFSpa.com.

---

## WESTGLOW SPA
### Blowing Rock, North Carolina

Built in 1916 as a summer home for artist Elliott Daingerfield, Westglow was converted into a spa in 1991. While the accommodations are historic, the spa's Life Enhancement Center is fitness forward. The spa's emphasis is clearly on stress reduction, life enhancement, and weight management through counseling, exercise, and old-fashioned relaxation. Its fitness and therapy facilities are state of the art, and its staff expertly trained and knowledgeable. Counseling doesn't stop at the front door, either. Guests can prepare for making healthy choices in real-world situations, for instance, by taking a practice shopping trip with a nutritionist to a local grocery store. Advice is also offered on how to prepare spa-style cuisine at home.

Rather than being named for its owner like many Victorian manors, Westglow's name refers to the extraordinary sunsets that grace the main veranda each evening. Watching the light and colors of the day change from the cyclorama of this hilltop setting can be an inspiring, if not urging backdrop for bringing about change in our own bodies and life outlooks.

**Season**    Year-round.
**Environs**    The Carolinas stretch of the Blue Ridge Mountains.
**Accommodations**    Bedroom suites in the manor house, plus two private cottages.
**Activities and Services**    Indoor swimming pool, Jacuzzi, wet

and dry saunas, aerobics studio, tennis, weight training, walking trails, croquet court. Nail- and hair-care salons. Spa services include nutritional counseling, tour of a grocery store with a nutritionist, body wraps, massages, facials.

**Religious Affiliation**    None.

**Rates**    Three days $1,294; four days $1,714; five days $2,108; seven days $2,772.

**For More Information**    Westglow Spa, P.O. Box 1083, U.S. Highway 221 S, Blowing Rock, N.C. 28605; phone (800) 562-0807; Website: www.westglow.com.

---

## WHOLISTIC LIFE CENTER
## Washburn, Missouri

This small lakeside retreat in the Ozark wilderness is an outreach ministry of the Wholistic Life Church, a nonprofit, nonsectarian organization. It operates as a kind of psychoreligious clinic and training program for reducing stress, improving diet and overall health, as well as breaking bad habits. The peaceful scenery, natural foods, and summer camp environment offer a setting conducive to letting go of patterns of thought and behavior that can hold you back in life both emotionally and physically.

The center's wide range of programs and services include dance, fitness and movement classes, nutritional guidance, lectures on naturopathy and universal ecology, chiropractic care, massage therapy, and creativity exercises, as well as dream analysis and pastoral counseling. Some workshops can be an emotional and spiritual challenge. For recreation, the center offers hiking, basketball, tennis, volleyball, and—for when the activity gets to be too much—hot tubs and massage.

**Season**   Year-round.

**Environs**   Nine hundred rolling acres of Ozark country, with lakes and trails for walking and climbing. Local air transportation is available at Fayetteville, Missouri, and the Northwest Arkansas Regional Airport.

**Accommodations**   Semiprivate cabins by the lake; meals are served family-style three times daily.

**Activities and Services**   Three-, seven-, and fourteen-day workshops on topics such as health and healing, discovery, inner beauty and rejuvenation, and the child within. Exercise and movement classes, hydrotherapy, chiropractic care, massage.

**Religious Affiliation**   Non-sectarian Christian.

**Rates**   A 501(c)(3) tax-exempt nonprofit organization, the center operates solely on donations. The suggested donation for a one-week program is $850 ($525 students); two-week $1,600 ($1,050 students); weekend workshops $395 ($225 students).

**For More Information**   Wholistic Life Center, Route 1 Box 1783, Washburn, Mo. 65772; phone (417) 435-2212; fax (417) 435-2216; Website: www.wholisticlifecenter.org.

---

## WILDWOOD LIFESTYLE CENTER AND HOSPITAL
## Wildwood, Georgia

Wildwood has one of the country's most outstanding programs for achieving and maintaining weight loss and good health. Run by Seventh-Day Adventists who keep a very low profile about their doctrine, Wildwood is centered on a belief in the body as temple. For more than forty years, its guests have learned to treat themselves better through instruction in nutrition, stress management, cooking, and exercise.

A miniumum ten- or seventeen-day stay is needed to allow time for positive results. Both programs include a physical

exam and blood chemistry, periodic physical consultations, vegetarian cooking classes, hydrotherapy, Jacuzzi and sauna, massage therapy, health lectures, and wholesome, nutritious meals. Morning spiritual lessons are offered by the center's full-time chaplain only if guests choose to attend. Many do not, and that's okay. The intimacy and support of no more than twenty fellow program participants, as well as the Wildwood recipe of clean air, exercise, water, sunshine, rest, and trust in others, will undoubtedly contribute to your own mental, spiritual, and physical health.

On average, guests lose one pound per day. But it's not only overweight people who have something to gain from the Wildwood diet and lifestyle: The program also caters to chronic sufferers of allergies, arthritis, and even depression. Other areas of repeated success are in the areas of preventive

medicine for heart disease, hypertension, diabetes, and cancer. Guests can expect significant reductions in blood pressure, as well as cholesterol and triglyceride levels and blood sugar (for diabetics). Since lifestyle changes are more likely to stick with the support and participation of others at home, guests can bring along a family member at a 20 percent discount. Finally, of special mention is the smoke-cessation seminar.

**Season**   Year-round.
**Environs**   Mountainside acres of fragrant southern pines in northern Georgia, with miles of well-kept trails and a lake for swimming. The center is convenient to Knoxville or Atlanta via I-75, and Nashville or Birmingham via I-24.

**Accommodations**   Shared rooms (each with two twin beds); private rooms when available. No televisions, and radios are allowed with headphones only. Also to promote tranquility, phones are absent from guest rooms but can be installed on request (a $25 deposit is required).

**Activities and Services**   Outdoor and indoor exercise, cooking classes, health lectures, hydrotherapy, massage, Jacuzzi, and sauna. Special seminars on nutrition, stress management, natural remedies, and smoke cessation.

**Religious Affiliation**   Seventh-Day Adventist, but no religious affiliation is required of program participants. The center is also a part of Wildwood Hospital, a top-notch medical facility dedicated to preventive medicine.

**Rates**   Ten-day program $1,740; seventeen-day $2,675; this includes lodging, meals, physical examination, physician consultations, and just about everything else. Claims can be submitted to your insurance company on request but, since many companies do not cover wellness programs, Wildwood cannot guarantee payment.

**For More Information**   Wildwood Lifestyle Center and Hospital, P.O. Box 129, Wildwood, Ga. 30757-0129; phone (800) 634-9355; Website: www.tagnet.org/Wildwood.

---

## WISDOM HOUSE RETREAT AND CONFERENCE CENTER
**Litchfield, Connecticut**

Formerly the home of a community of Catholic sisters, these fifty-four acres in the hills of northwestern Connecticut now serve as an interfaith center for women and men seeking an environment for learning and contemplation. Meadows, woods, brooks, and quiet country roads are dotted with indoor and outdoor sanctuaries for meditation, prayer, and creative thinking. Overnight retreatants and Connecticut residents can take part in ongoing evening classes such as Universal Soul Singing, Sitting in Silence, or sessions of Kripalu and Hatha yoga.

Guests reside in a circa-1770 stark white farmhouse with a fireplace for the winter months and enclosed porch for spring and summer, or in the more conventlike cubicle rooms of a brick, Colonial-style building. Special retreats are offered for writers and artists, and there is even an art gallery on the premises.

**Season**   Year-round.

**Environs**   New England scenery, most wonderful during the fall when leaves are turning. It's about forty-five miles from Bridgeport (Connecticut), thirty miles from Hartford, seventy miles from Albany, and one hundred miles from New York City.

**Accommodations**   Accommodations are based on shared bedrooms, unless otherwise indicated, and include meals (generally vegetarian). A limited number of private rooms is available on request.

**Activities and Services**   Classes and programs centering on spiritual health and creative living. Hiking, swimming, and time for individual reflection.

**Religious Affiliation**   Roman Catholic, but retreatants of any faith are welcome.

**Rates**   Very inexpensive; please remember to be generous and add $15 per night for private accommodations. Suggested donations for evening classes average about $6; please call for special programs and costs.

**For More Information**   Wisdom House, 229 East Litchfield Road, Litchfield, Conn. 06759-3002; phone (860) 567-3163; fax (860) 567-3166; e-mail: info@wisdomhouse.org.

## WISE WOMAN CENTER
## Woodstock, New York

Wise Woman Center founder Susan S. Weed is a witch. Not
the kind with a black pointy hat and broom, but a green witch
who uses herbs and weeds for healing. Her center teaches
others to share in the wisdom of the earth and their bodies
through herbal medicine, women's spirituality, and meditation.
Programs are generally for women only, but some two- and
four-day intensive workshops are open to men as well.

Workshop types include an Herbal Intensive, Spirit Healing Intensive, Sacred Sex, Transformational Healing, and a
special course designed to Awaken the Wise Woman and
Wizard Within. Guests gather in circles, sing, dance, and take
turns passing the talking stick. Every now and then, a pair of
laughing goats will butt in on the fun. Visiting speakers enjoy
notoriety in their fields; notable herbalists, priestesses, witches,
and healers have included Vicki Noble and Z Budapest, and
feminist performance artist Annie Sprinkle (she co-instructed
a seminar on sacred sex).

Daylong workshops (from 10 A.M. to 5 P.M.) are also available. Herbal Medicine Chest instructs you on how to replace
common drugstore medicines with natural cures; Spirit Healing
Skills is an introduction to chanting, toning, and shamanic journeys; and a special course for menopausal women familiarizes
them with their herbal allies for strong bones and sensuality.

**Season**  Scheduled workshops run year-round.
**Environs**  Located in upstate New York between legendary
Woodstock and Saugerties, a town of historic homes and
antiques shops, the center is accessible by car, bus, and air-
plane (from Albany or Newburgh).

**Accommodations**   Guests should bring a sleeping bag to sleep in tents, in a tepee, or indoors. Vegetarian meals are included in the cost.

**Activities and Services**   Herbal medicine and women's spirituality intensives. Hiking, swimming, and shamanic journeys.

**Religious Affiliation**   Teachings are informed by the Jewish, Catholic, Christian, Buddhist, and Wiccan faiths.

**Rates**   Sliding-scale rates depending on personal finances; some work exchange and barter are available.

**For More Information**   Wise Woman Center, P.O. Box 64, Woodstock, N.Y. 12498; phone and fax (914) 246-8081.

# PART TWO

◆

# FIRE

*You are a King by your own Fireside*
*as much as any Monarch in his Throne*

— MIGUEL DE CERVANTES,
in his preface to *Don Quixote*

# FIRE

◆

Fire can be hard for many of us to conceive of as an element. It strikes us more as a force, full of mystery and primal energy. In Greek myth, fire was reserved for the gods alone until Prometheus dared to sneak up on Mount Olympus and steal away with a few embers for mankind. Men and women seeking its powers of warmth, light, and divinity have had the challenge of harnessing fire ever since.

Unleashed, fire can annihilate a landscape. Contain it and fire can dispel darkness, disperse coldness, and ignite our senses. It can transform a substance—witness fuel consumed—or purify on contact. A knife passed through flames is sterilized. One small lighted match can rid an entire room of lingering smells.

Fire, for all its danger, is also a positive catalyst, creating pathways between the known and the unknown. It is the single mediating element between light and dark, the visible and the invisible. Ancient visionaries looked into the movement of fire to see the future, Native Americans danced around its flames to call forth spirits, and we blow out candles on a birthday cake believing some unknown entity will grant our wish.

Alchemists held that fire was an agent of transmutation that could turn anything to gold. Fire vacations can be similarly enriching for those of us seeking personal transformation. You've probably felt the warmth of the sun on your skin during vacation before; this time around, you'll feel it radiate from you. Fire vacations focus on internal energies. They bring on change from the inside out, surging your passions, increasing your zest and ambitions. They can help you burn away perceived obstacles and self-doubt. Like the Phoenix rising reborn from the ashes, you can hope to leave these various places and adventures feeling not just renewed, but in exalted form.

---

## ALCHEMY INSTITUTE OF HEALING ARTS
## (Formerly the Alchemical Hypnotherapy Institute)
## Santa Rosa, California

The concept of alchemical hypnotherapy is based on a synthesis of modern psychology and ancient practices such as shamanism and alchemy as translated into modern thought by Carl Jung. The process strives to understand and harness actions of the subconscious mind through "alert trance" hypnosis. Founder David Quigley promotes alchemical hypnotherapy as a way to put us in touch with our Inner Guides, described as autonomous beings living within our subconscious with the power to release us from past pain and neglect and guide us to health, happiness, and the fulfillment of our spiritual purpose on earth.

People come to the institute to train as alchemical professionals, but retreatants content with their own careers are also welcome. Workshops help guests quit smoking, manage their weight, or cope better with stress as well as deal with the very serious issues of addiction recovery, child abuse, and molestation. A natural part of the process, alchemical hypnotherapy also helps guests enhance their creative and career potential.

Retreats are limited to fifteen people. The institute also runs off-site weekend training courses in hotels and Wilderness Intensives for the public. Another option is its Empowerment Intensive experiences, which combine alchemical hypnotherapy with psychodrama, movement, music, and ceremony to produce a truly profound healing experience for the body, mind, and spirit.

**Season** The institute is open year-round, but retreats and workshops for the public are scheduled. Please call for latest calendar of on- and off-site offerings.

**Environs** Programs are not site specific.

**Accommodations** These vary according to program location (typically held at resorts in Pacific and Southwestern states, as well as in cities of Atlanta, Salt Lake City, and Chicago).

**Activities and Services** Alchemical hypnotherapy; outdoor and creative activities as part of select programs.

**Religious Affiliation** None.

**Rates** Personal Growth Training: $1,320 plus registration and textbooks (also room and board if applicable). Sedona Wilderness Retreat: $875 including lodging and meals.

**For More Information** Alchemy Institute of Healing Arts, 567-A Summerfield Road, Santa Rosa, Calif. 95405; phone (800) 950-4984 or (outside the United States) (707) 537-0495; fax (707) 537-0496; Website: www.hollys.com/alchemy.

---

## ASHRAM HEALTH RETREAT
## Calabasas, California

Though the cost is reasonable and the experience anything but luxurious, the Ashram attracts a fairly affluent crowd. Guests range in age from twenty to seventy, and their vocations vary from supermodel and actor to midwestern executive. But in at least one respect, they are all alike. They are achievers by nature, attached to their high-pressure jobs and not likely to reach Nirvana locked inside a flotation tank or wallowing under layers of Calistoga mud. Feeling stressed out and unable to relax but very much hoping for some kind of transcendent experience, these men and women fare better on a vacation where they can put their drive and ambitions to a more internal test. The Ashram Health Retreat serves them as a type of spiritual boot camp, upping their perceived limits through vigorous exercise and stark diet.

Ashram founder and director Dr. Anne Marie Bennstrom understands her guests because she is like them. A Swedish-born former cross-country skiing champion, well-known aerobics pioneer, and licensed chiropractor, she gained a reputation in the United States teaching at a Hollywood gym in the early 1970s. She moved on to the Golden Door and later became proprietor of the Sanctuary, where she met her current partner, Ashram Associate Director Catharina Hedberg. Called Cat, Ms. Hedberg is a graduate cum laude of the University of Stockholm in physical medicine and physical education.

Together, these two women have designed a very intense physical fitness program that effectively combines the camaraderie of group activity with attention to individual needs. The day starts at 6:30 A.M. with yoga followed by a light (virtually nonexistent) breakfast. At 8:30 A.M., it's time to set out on a five-hour hike in the mountains. Lunch is at two P.M., followed by fifty minutes of deep tissue massage described by one very sore-muscled guest as "blissful torture." At 3:30 P.M., the fun starts again with sessions of aerobic weight training and water exercise in the outdoor pool. Things wind down at about 5:30 with yoga and meditation. Dinner is vegetarian, comprising little more than cooked beans, vegetables, and grains. Evening programs (if you can stay awake) include lectures on energy balancing, developing healthy habits, and general spirituality. The day closes at 9 P.M. after one last session of meditation in the geodesic dome.

By the end of the week at Ashram, you'll have hiked seventy miles and rid yourself of impurities and toxins, as well as some pounds. At the very least you will be lighter in spirit. Maybe you'll have gained a new appreciation for mung beans, but more likely you will return home with the thrill of new friends, greater self-esteem, and knowledge of your fortitude in rising to life's challenges. And finally, as if the sense of personal triumph was not enough, you'll receive an I SURVIVED THE ASHRAM T-shirt.

**Season** Year-round.
**Environs** A secluded valley location surrounded by running streams and the Santa Monica Mountains. The Ashram is fifteen minutes from Malibu Beach and approximately one hour west of Los Angeles.
**Accommodations** Guests are assigned roommates (no exceptions) to share one of five bedrooms in a ranch house; shared bathrooms, library, lounge, and free weights room; exercise clothes and bathrobe provided. For the more adventurous, outdoor porch accommodations are available at a lower rate.
**Activities and Services** Outdoor exercise including swimming and water volleyball in the pool. Massage, nutritional counseling, yoga and meditation, and outdoor Jacuzzi. Evening lecture series on health and general spirituality.
**Religious Affiliation** None.
**Rates** A one-week stay is $2,500, meals and snacks included.
**For More Information** The Ashram, P.O. Box 8009, Calabasas, Calif. 91372; phone (818) 222-6900; e-mail: theashram@theashram.com; Website: www.theashram.com.

## What is Ayurveda?

Ayurveda (ah´-yoor-VEY-dah) is a five-thousand-year-old system of medicine native to India. It's based on the idea that all disease begins with an imbalance or stress in a person's consciousness. Since it's a mind-body connection that allows illness to occur, Ayurvedic methods focus on the nature of that connection. Unlike other holistic approaches to medicine, Ayurveda argues that we are each unique. Every one of us has a particular constitution and temperament, a mind-body network that's wired to make us look, react, eat, and sleep in typical patterns, and to be prone to associated kinds of illness.

What allows Ayurveda to treat individuals is not our outward symptoms, but its conviction that we all, more or less, fall into three categories of body-mind principles, or *doshas*, labeled *vata* (air), *pitta* (fire), and *kapha* (earth).

All three doshas rise and fall in everyone according to their own temperaments, as well as with the seasons, the time of day, and changes in the body. The goal of Ayurveda is to keep each person's dominant dosha in balance. Vatas (air), who are naturally lively and stimulated, should not go without sleep, be malnourished, or become overanxious; pittas (fire) — known for their sharp intellects, strong passions, and focused ambitions — should not throw temper tantrums or suffer from chronic heartburn; and kaphas (earth) should be their down-to-earth selves at ease in life situations without having to suffer under the weight of lethargy, depression, or physical congestion.

Ayurveda aims to prevent and treat illness through natural therapies, including oils, herbs, and the massage methods of the Vedic Scriptures, as well as through lifestyle interventions. Finding the right exercise, the right way to relax, the best foods, the choice music, colors, and scents for your home and office can choreograph those fluctuating doshas into perfect health. No matter what your dosha, the key elements of Ayurvedic living will involve moderation, meditation, some form of regular exercise, and contact with nature.

In India, Ayurveda is mainstream medicine. Its practitioners receive state-recognized, institutionalized training with a rigor much like that of their Western physician counterparts. Conventional medicine is now paying attention. The National Institutes of Health is currently funding research in this ancient science, with most studies focusing on the physiological effects of meditative techniques and yoga postures. Documented studies of Ayurvedic herbal preparations and other therapies have shown them to have a range of potentially beneficial effects in reducing cardiovascular disease risk factors (including blood pressure, cholesterol, and reaction to stress), as well as preventing and treating certain cancers, treating infectious disease, promoting health, and treating aging.

There are currently ten Ayurveda clinics in North America, including one hospital-based clinic. Ayurveda is also at the core of teachings by Deepak Chopra, best-selling author, New Age celebrity, and founder of the Chopra Center for Well Being in La Jolla, California.

---

## THE CHOPRA CENTER FOR WELL BEING
### La Jolla, California

The Chopra Center for Well Being is the brainchild of Dr. Deepak Chopra, the best-selling author on mind-body medicine and techniques for personal development. Between his publications and the New Age lecture circuit, Chopra is a busy man. He may be intimately involved in the center's operations, but the most you can expect to see of this wise, handsome, and very charismatic doctor are the publicity photos on his many books sold in the center's store. This isn't really a problem, though, because the institution runs on strong philosophical and medical principles, that have credibility far beyond the cult of any personality. Before it opened to the public, the Chopra Center operated as a research institute studying the effectiveness of Ayurvedic and Western medicine and the mind-body connection.

Ayurveda, the ancient healing tradition from India, is at the core of services offered at the Chopra Center. After arriving for a three- to seven-day program, you will be asked to fill out a questionnaire. Questions asked range from your appetite to your hair type, body temperature, eye size, what kind of climate you like best, and how you typically react under stress. The purpose is to discover your true nature (or *dosha*, in Ayurvedic lingo) and, consequently, the lifestyle choices and healing therapies that can raise your energies and boost your potential.

The most comprehensive programs last seven days and begin with an Ayurvedic medical consultation. From there your visit will take an individually prescribed course. A typical day goes like this: early-morning meditation, breakfast, yoga or breath classes, Primordial Sound Meditation instruction, lunch, massage, group meditation, dinner, and a class. Spa treatments can be enjoyed as part of a multiday program or à la carte; they range from traditional pampering to the especially exotic and luxurious. Spa beginners should try the special sampler of wonders called the Odyssey Massage, which offers a window onto the benefits of aromatherapy, Garshana, Abhyanga, Vishesh massage, and Vital Touch techniques. Pizichilli, a seventy-minute treatment, is a more intense experience during which two therapists pour a continuous stream of warm herbal oil over your body, then rhythmically massage along the path of the oil's flow.

Specialty five-day programs include lifestyle courses on finding your perfect weight, healing your heart, and emotional wholeness, along with a Return to Wholeness Cancer Program and a Women's Week. Depending on your choice of focus, you can learn about nutrition and herbs; how to increase your strength through yoga and exercise; how to boost your energy, reduce stress, and enhance creativity through meditation, visualization, or art therapy; and even how to improve your communication skills to reach personal and career goals. What these achievements are all about is taking a more active role in your own well-being. The goal is to leave for home using your senses more fully in an enlivened connection between body, mind, emotions, and spirit.

**Season**  Year-round programs.

**Environs**  Near the Pacific Ocean in southern California.

**Accommodations**  Programs range from three to seven days, but no overnight accommodations are available. Guests stay at nearby hotels, varying from luxurious to inexpensive. Dining is full-service gourmet vegetarian, with natural cooking classes available.

**Rates**  Three-day packages, including Ayurvedic consultations and panchakarma treatments from $1,300 to $1,750; five-day from $2,300 to $2,550. Spa treatments taken à la carte can cost up to $200 per hour. Breakfast, lunch, and dinner are included with program costs and scheduled into your day at the center.

**Activities and Services**  Daily group meditation and yoga; Primordial Sound Meditation and Healing Breath instruction. Comprehensive initial physician visit, health classes, Ayurvedic nurse consultations. Panchakarma and other massage therapies, Ayurvedic and other body- and skin-care treatments. Aromatherapy, emotional cleansing and processing, movement and art therapy.

**Religious Affiliation**    None.

**Of Special Mention**    The physician-visit portion of your program may be covered by your health-insurance policy; check with your provider before arrival, because only select policies cover spa treatments. Copies of results from lab tests run no more than three months prior to arrival are recommended in the case of persistent medical conditions.

**For More Information**    The Chopra Center for Well Being, 7630 Fay Avenue, La Jolla, Calif. 92037; phone (619) 551-7788 or (888) 424-6772; fax (619) 551-7811 or 9750; e-mail: info@chopra.com; Website: www.chopra.com.

---

## GOLDEN DOOR
## Escondido, California

The Golden Door opens onto a vitalizing lifestyle. Geared exclusively to women forty-three weeks out of the year (with five men only and four coed weeks annually), its fitness programs and meditative surroundings are designed to help guests trade in their lethargy for energy.

Located eight miles north of Escondido (Spanish for "hidden"), the resort is intensely intimate: Only thirty-nine guests can visit at any one time. Luxury exists not only in the services but in the details, from the fragrances in the air to fresh-cut flowers and Japanese art and antiques in your room. There are also meticulously landscaped grounds, exquisite food presentation, and the ever-present humming of streams, waterfalls, and fountains. Such details add greatly to your understanding that you are well cared for, safe from decision making

or other external obstacles, and free to aspire past your perceived physical and mental limits.

As exclusive as vacations at Golden Door sound, the atmosphere is surprisingly unassuming. The uniform white robes, exercise clothes, and kimonos the spa provides to each guest do much to wear down elitist pretensions and encourage more wholly enriching pursuits.

Also, a great deal is possible when the ratio of staff to guests is 4:1. With this degree of supervision, all guests can be assured of a program tailored to fit their individual needs. Guests arrive on a Sunday and are assigned a personal exercise guide who, after a preliminary evaluation, guides them through a daily fitness regimen and charts their progress. The intensity of morning exercise sessions increases incrementally all week long, but these alternate with hours reserved for pampering or other quieting pursuits. You can tour meditative gardens, take a class in t'ai chi or Hatha yoga, or walk a replica of the classical floor labyrinth laid in Chartres Cathedral at the outset of the thirteenth century.

Each day brings new surprises. No two sunrise hikes are the same, and every afternoon offers a different spa service or treatment, chosen by you at the recommendation of your own personal aesthetician. Enjoy a seductive selection of facials, or exotic body treatments such as seaweed thalassotherapy or Moor mud therapy. Evenings are occupied by lectures, crafts classes, or informal cooking instruction with the spa chef. Only bedtime is a ritual: A dip in a hot Japanese tub and a comforting mini massage usher in restful nights of sleep.

Of special mention is the Inner Door Program, a mind-body-spirit development retreat for those already physically fit, as well as those special weeks (and rates!) reserved for mothers and daughters, or fathers and sons.

**Season**    Year-round; closed Christmas week.

**Environs**    Secluded coastal southern Californian location on 177 acres of meadows and hilltops. The scenery includes orange and avocado groves, mountain lilacs, and Oriental gardens. Golden Door is thirty miles north of San Diego (with a courtesy shuttle to and from San Diego's Lindbergh Field airport).

**Accommodations**    Single rooms in Japanese *honjin*-style inns, decorated with Japanese wood-block prints, sliding shoji screens, and jalousie windows; each includes a sitting area opening onto a garden. Three high-energy, low-cholesterol meals and snacks are served daily.

**Activities and Services**    Twenty miles of hiking trails, indoor exercise facilities, two outdoor pools, tennis courts. Instruction in t'ai chi, Hatha yoga, aerobics, swimming, nutrition and cooking, and stress management. Spa services include a variety of massage techniques, aromatherapy, body scrubs, facials, and herbal wraps; sauna, steam room, Swiss shower, and whirlpool available.

**Religious Affiliation**   None.

**Rates**   The fee is $5,000 weekly; $4,500 during off-peak summer months (from June 14 to September 6) and holidays (Thanksgiving and New Year's weeks). Daily beauty treatments and massage are included in cost; there are additional fees for tennis and crafts instruction only.

**For More Information**   Golden Door, Deer Springs Road, Box 463077, Escondido, Calif. 92046; phone (800) 414-0777 or (619) 744-5777; fax (619) 471-2393; Website: www.goldendoor.com.

---

## KALANI HONUA CONFERENCE AND RETREAT CENTER
## Pahoa, Hawaii

Kalani means "heavenly" in Hawaiian, and while the location certainly is, this resort is for the curious and budget conscious rather than the spoiled and pampered. At a coastal point with area beaches, nearby thermal springs, and natural steam baths, this intercultural conference center makes use of its spectacular setting to provide its guests with activities relating to the physical, spiritual, and emotional healing arts as well as traditional Hawaiian culture. Daily offerings include a dizzying spectrum of group workshops and conferences (the selection is always changing), but vacationers should look to the center's wellness retreats.

At Kalani's Oceanside Retreat, you can not only experience but also learn Hawaiian lomilomi massage and floating shiatsu (Watsu). Other retreats focus on reiki (healing with life energy), t'ai chi, hula, and yoga, or topics such as Vision and Intuition or Living From the Heart. A special women's seminar for encountering Hawaii's own volcanic goddess titled Into the Womb of Pele combines adventure with women's spirituality. An on-site Japanese-style spa offers therapeutic services and exercise classes, and a wooden bathhouse contains a communal hot tub, wood-heated sauna, and private massage rooms.

**Season**   Year-round; The high season is from mid-December to the end of April.

**Environs**   Five miles from the lava flow of Mount Kilauea on the Puna Coast of the Big Island of Hawaii.

**Accommodations**   Double- or multiple-occupancy rooms in cedar lodges decorated with Hawaiian flowers, prints, and fabrics; shared baths. Meals are offered à la carte, or by daily meal plan; there's also a communal kitchen for guest use. Some private cottages are available, as well as tent sites.

**Activities and Services**   Hiking, picnics, beach frolicking, outdoor pool, cycling, volleyball; golf and skiing are nearby. Reiki, yoga (mostly Kripalu and Hatha), t'ai chi, dance (including hula). Services include massage, acupressure and acupuncture, Watsu, chiropractic.

**Religious Affiliation**   None.

**Rates**   High-season singles run $90 to $110, doubles $110 to $130; low-season singles are $75 to $90, doubles $95 to $110.

**For More Information**   Kalani Oceanside Retreat, R.R. 2 Box 4500, Pahoa-Beach Road, Hawaii 96778; phone (800) 800-6886 or (808) 965-7828; fax (808) 965-9613; e-mail: kalani@kalani.com; Website: www.kalani.com.

## KARMÊ CHÖLING AND THE THREE GATES OF SHAMBHALA
**Barnet, Vermont**

A center for Buddhist meditation, Karmê Chöling ("tail of the tiger") is an attractive retreat set on 540 acres of meadows and woodlands. Buildings and gardens fuse New England, Tibetan, and Japanese design elements. Leading from the center, a dirt road winds up the hill with six small shrines along the way. At the top is an open field with an outdoor shrine where hundreds gather during the summer months for special events.

Chögyam Trungpa founded the place in 1970, and it is primarily his teachings that retreatants explore today. The center's namesake Three Gates are the three ways of reaching Buddhist enlightenment and, accordingly, the center offers instruction in each: Vajradhatu, Shambhala, and Nalanda.

Vajradhatu is inspired by the Kagyü and Nyingma traditions of Tibetan Buddhism. Students aspiring to this gate learn basic meditation practices, then follow a clearly defined path of solitary retreats, study programs, ngöndro practices, empowerments, and fire offerings.

Shambhala training teaches that there is a basic human wisdom found in all cultures and traditions that can help solve the world's problems. Called human warriorship, this tradition of wisdom is the subject of programs of increasing levels of commitment. The Heart of Warriorship Program (levels I to V) helps individuals establish a personal meditation discipline intended to bring principles of warriorship, gentleness, fearlessness, and precision into daily life. Advanced Sacred Path of the Warrior Programs (levels A, W, B, C, D, and Golden Key) profoundly deepen participants' practice and study of the Shambhala teachings.

The Nalanda Gate requires a more contemplative approach, and is represented at Karmê Chöling by classes in the arts, health, psychology, social issues, family, relationships, business, and education.

Beginning and advanced practitioners of Buddhist meditation are welcome. Parents are especially invited on weekends and holidays, when programs for teens and children are held. Programs vary in length from two days to one month.

**Season**   Year-round.

**Environs**   Beautiful, green Vermont. Located a half mile off I-91 (exit 18), about one hour north of White River Junction. Local airports are Lebanon, New Hampshire, and Burlington, Vermont; the Dartmouth Mini Coach (800-637-0123 or 603-448-2800) provides shuttle service from the Boston airport.

**Accommodations**   Dormitory beds ($5 a night), single or double rooms ($25 to $35 a night) in 6 retreat cabins and a charming guesthouse in nearby Barnet; bring your own bedding. Tent sites are also available ($5 a night), and for non-campers willing to rough it, program participants are welcome to sleep on foam mats in the large meditation hall for no additional fee. Call for weekly and monthly rates. Meals are taken cafeteria-style.

**Activities and Services**   Meditation instruction; classes in Kyudo (archery), Ikebana (flower arranging), Chado (tea ceremony), Shodo (calligraphy), as well as Maitri Space Awareness Practice, Dharma Art, Buddhist psychology, health and well-being, wealth and livelihood, and family programs.

**Religious Affiliation**   Tibetan Buddhist (Kagyü and Nyingma lineages) and Shambhala teachings.

**Rates**   Sliding-scale program fees from $85, cost of accommodations separate. There's a 20% discount off program fees for seniors, full-time students, and Canadians. A $50 deposit must accompany all program registrations, cost of one night deposit upon confirmation of private room.

**For More Information**   Karmê Chöling Buddhist Meditation Center, R.R. 1 Box 3, Barnet, Vt. 05821; phone (802) 633-2384; fax (802) 633-3012; e-mail: KarmeCholing@Shambala.org; Website:www.kcl.shambala.org.

---

## MAHARISHI AYUR-VEDA MEDICAL CENTER
### Lancaster, Massachusetts

The Maharishi Center describes what it does as consciousness-based health care. It offers exceedingly intimate programs for rejuvenation and prevention of illness. Operating from the Ayurvedic perspective that health is attained by creating and maintaining balance in the mind and body, its programs make real the benefits of yoga, regular exercise, an organic vegetarian diet, herbal preparations, and transcendental meditation.

The center's approach to health is enjoyable. Panchakarma spa treatments are purely physical, often sensuous. On a very basic level, the comforts they induce generate a healing influence. Taken in a specific sequence, however, these treatments can gently purify the body of accumulated toxins. But that's only the beginning. Maharishi claims that flushing your body of toxins can actually help reverse the effects of aging. The center explains this in terms of a principle called *shrota shuddi*, which is Sanskrit for "purification of body channels." Removing blockages to the flow of biological intelligence through these channels can have an energizing effect on the mind. It can also help the body strengthen its immunity and thereby restore its physiology to a balanced, natural state of being.

How is all this done? At the Maharishi Center, panchakarma treatments include Abhyanga (full-body herbalized oil massage), shirodhara (cool oil or milk poured onto the forehead), and pindaswedana (full-body massage with rice balls and herbal packs), as well as steam baths, nasal congestion therapy, and deep tissue massage.

Programs at the center can focus on rejuvenation, on spiritual development, or on vitality. Each experience is tailored to your own needs as determined in consultation with your resident physician, trained in both Western and Ayurvedic medicines. In-depth programs are also offered for chronic conditions ranging from acne to headaches, allergies, menstrual problems, obesity, and even depression.

**Season**   Year-round.

**Environs**   A redbrick mansion on a rolling green lawn in a rural New England setting.

**Accommodations**   Elegant rooms in the ten-guest mansion house; organic vegetarian gourmet meals are provided.

**Activities and Services**   Ayurvedic medicine and treatments, yoga, transcendental meditation, nature walks.

**Religious Affiliation**   None.

**Rates**   Programs range from $3,200 to $4,500 per person per week.

**For More Information**   Maharishi Ayur-Veda Medical Center, 679 George Hill Road, Lancaster, Mass. 01523; phone (978) 365-4549; fax (978) 368-7557.

---

## THE MERRIT CENTER
**Payson, Arizona**

Betty and Al Merrit founded this forest hideaway as a non-profit adult education center for self-realization and empowerment. At its heart is a sweat lodge; Betty is the lodge keeper. Trained in rites by a Cheyenne-Arapaho, she now imbues her own lodge ceremonies with anything from Buddhist and Tibetan chants to popular Sunday-school anthems and campfire songs.

The sweat lodge is a ceremony in itself, but can also be part of a larger learning experience. For instance, on two different weekend programs—Women's Journey and Crossroads, a vision quest–like journey for men and women—the lodge is used on Saturday evening, at the peak of intimacy and learning. Inside the lodge, heat rises from rocks scented with fragrant grass or cedar. As the vapors rise and heat seeps into muscles, minds also relax. Cleansing begins when participants drop inhibitions by revealing secrets and speaking their prayers out loud.

If chanting and drumming are not your thing, other worthwhile classes in personal growth include couples' enrichment, community building, art therapy, and meditation. Other visitors opt out of the classes and focus on activities such as t'ai chi, nature walks, stargazing, and yoga. The Heart Renewal Program helps individuals evaluate their lifestyles and learn healthier alternatives in nutrition, exercise, communication skills, and emotional support structures.

Programs are very reasonably priced and intimate (limited to twenty-two participants). During 1999, the Merrit Center offered three programs affiliated with Elderhostel, the nationwide, nonprofit educational network serving adults fifty-five and over.

**Season**   Year-round.

**Environs**   This rustic lodge, at an elevation of five thousand feet among tall ponderosa pines, is ninety miles north of Phoenix, near the Mogollon Rim.

**Accommodations**   Double-occupancy rooms; private and shared baths.

**Activities and Services**   Nature hikes, t'ai chi, hot tub, Kiatsu bodywork, Swedish massage, Native American sweat lodge.

**Religious Affiliation**   None.

**Rates**   Single accommodations $75 to $125 (low season), or $100 to $150 (high season); doubles $110 to $170 (low season), or $120 to $185 (high season).

**For More Information**   Merrit Lodge of Payson, P.O. Box 2087, Payson, Ariz. 85547-2087; phone (520) 474-4268.

## ORBIS FARM
## Mauckport, Indiana

A farm of vitality rather than crops or livestock, Orbis Farm is a seventy-five-acre track of woodland with only a few acres cleared for its retreat houses and gardens. Owned and operated by two sisters, it offers intimate yet affordable yoga and meditative weekend retreats accommodating from six to twenty guests.

The specialty here is Kundalini meditation. Based on the Sanskrit word for "coiled up," this form of yoga and meditation aims to release our evolutionary energy force. The goddess Kundalini is believed to linger coiled three and a half times around the base of our spines; unwound little by little, Kundalini energy can push us to greater creativity, sharpen our mental powers, enhance our sensitivity to people and nature, and, ultimately, lead to enlightenment. Stirring up Kundalini without instruction, however, is a little like playing with fire. Yes, folklore puts Kundalini energy at the center of genius, but it also sees it at the core of various forms of insanity. Through intensive courses of attentive instruction, retreatants learn how this volatile force can be harnessed, explored, and understood to bring greater awareness, enhanced skills, and gifts.

Guests walk a replica of a classical labyrinth, circling and stopping at junctures (corresponding to compass points on the North American Indian medicine wheel) to perform a ritual honoring the energy of that place along their centrifugal path. What better metaphor for releasing a coiled goddess?

Other programs at Orbis Farm include more general yoga training, work in a "co-creative" garden (organic, of course), and a two-part consciousness-raising retreat called the Heroine's Journey, cotaught by a licensed psychologist and a meditation instructor.

**Season**    Open from the last weekend in January to the first weekend in November (closed December).

**Environs**    Wooded acres located in the southernmost tip of Indiana, forty miles west of Louisville, Kentucky.

**Accommodations**    Two dorms, one for men and the other for women, both with central heating, air-conditioning, and shared bathrooms. Bedding is supplied.

**Activities and Services**    Yoga and Kundalini meditation, gardening, hiking, and a hot tub on the porch.

**Religious Affiliation**    None.

**Rates**    The cost is $180 for a weekend retreat, beginning with dinner on Friday and ending with lunch on Sunday afternoon. This includes all instruction, meals, and lodging.

**For More Information**    Orbis Farm, 8700 Ripperdan Valley Road SW, Mauckport, Ind. 47142; phone (812) 732-4657.

─────────────

## THE ORCHID AT MAUNA LANI
### Kohala Coast, Hawaii

Touting its location at one of a handful of mystical "power points" on the planet, the Orchid at Mauna Lani offers healthful vacations sure to fill your cravings for physical wellness, psychic rejuvenation, romance, and good old-fashioned adventurous family fun.

Nearby lies Kilauea, the world's most active volcano, where the fiery goddess Pele is believed to reside; the Puako Petroglyph Preserve, one of the largest concentrations of these ancient lava bed drawings, is also close. Mauna Lani guides will take you on hikes through these historic locales or on more rigorous canoeing, kayaking, and snorkeling adventures. Or you can stick to the brisk, but not too arduous, sunrise power walk.

The Center for Well Being is the resort's full-service spa, offering a wonderful range of massage therapies (oceanside or inside) and body treatments (featuring Native Hawaiian healing plants) as well as movement classes (t'ai chi, qi gong, yoga, mandala meditation, and hula classes). Of special mention are the lomilomi massage, an ancient technique set to the rhythm of Polynesian drums, and the Body Temple Lomi Massage, traditionally used for ceremonial purposes. Couples are welcome to learn massage techniques in the Art of Massage class, and there is a specially designed Golfer's Massage. Much more than relaxing is Super Body/Mind Synchronization, which combines therapeutic massage techniques with electronic brain wave stimulation for mind-expanding effects. Hypnotherapy is particularly helpful for those feeling a mental block of some kind; also recommended are the therasound and craniosacral therapies.

Use of the high-tech fitness center is free for all guests, with personal trainers, fitness consultations, and body composition analysis available for a fee. While you're working out, your kids and teens can enjoy any of a variety of beachside activities, from shell hunts and cave explorations to Hawaiian crafts and language classes.

But what would a Hawaiian resort holiday be without a game of golf? Sign up for the holistic version of the game, Whole in One, and you'll learn to improve your game through focusing techniques aimed at balancing mental and physical forces. Instruction in the art of muscular imagination should enhance your fluidity of movement and even improve your control of the ball.

**Season**   Year-round.

**Environs**   The sun-drenched Kohala Coast on the volcanic island of Hawaii, home to white beaches, crystal blue waters, and sacred sites.

**Accommodations**   Rooms and suites in a luxury two-story resort hotel, each with private terrace, marble bath, and grooming essentials.

**Activities and Services**   Historic hikes, golf (Francis H. Brown thirty-six-hole championship course), tennis, horseback riding, snorkeling, two lava-enhanced whirlpools, full-service spa, fitness center. Programs for children and teens; baby-sitting available.

**Religious Affiliation**   None.

**Rates**   The cost varies depending on package type and room occupancy; fees can range upward of $500 per day.

**For More Information**   The Orchid at Mauna Lani, One North Kaniku Drive, Kohala Coast, Hawaii 96743; phone (808) 885-2000 or (800) 845-9905; fax (808) 885-5778; Website: www.orchid-maunalani.com.

---

## THE MODERN MEDICINE OF PRAYER

Signs on the property of Our Lady of Solitude House of Prayer high in the Sonoran Desert read, NO SMOKING EXCEPT FOR THE FIRE OF PRAYER. Fire in this instance may be a metaphor for power or passion but, as even modern science attests, a transfer of energy can indeed occur during deep prayer that has the power to heal.

According to the National Institutes of Health, a number of experiments have documented the influence that humans can exhibit on a variety of cellular and biological systems through mental means alone. Bacteria, yeasts, fungi, plants, insects, chicks, mice, rats, gerbils, cats, dogs—all kinds of living things not open to the powers of suggestion—have been influenced by outside mental activity, and their blood cells, neurons, cancer cells, and enzyme activities have been affected. Targeted human subjects have likewise exhibited change in muscular movements, electrodermal activity, plethysmographic activity, respiration, and brain rhythms. The energy of healing thoughts works over distance, too, with results occurring even when the person targeted for influence was unaware of the efforts being made.

While it's true that these scientific studies don't go so far as to describe the intentions of the influencer as "prayer," there's no denying that participants assumed a prayerful state characterized by genuine feelings of caring, compassion, love, empathy, or a feeling that they were "one" with the subject of their entreaties.

## PECOS BENEDICTINE MONASTERY
### Pecos, New Mexico

Saint Benedict once said we should receive all guests as we would Christ himself, and ever since receiving visitors has been a tenet of Benedictine monasticism. This monastery, nestled into a picturesque New Mexican river valley at seven thousand feet, not only accommodates guests for private retreats, but plans weeks of directed retreat during which guests can partake in activities blending both sacred and psychological methods of healing. These include dream interpretation in the biblical tradition, enneagram study with contemplative prayer, and a special retreat for Healing the Family Tree. Marriage encounters and family retreats are a consistent focus of the retreat ministry. Since its introduction here in 1969, charismatic renewal has also been a touchstone of life at the monastery. Emphasizing personal religious experience and divinely inspired powers, charismatic retreats can entail healing, prophecy, and the gift of tongues (Pentecostal fire).

Pecos is a double monastery, consisting of one family in two distinct communities, male (Mother of Mercy and Peace Monastery) and female (Our Lady of Guadalupe Abbey). While guided retreats are offered here, you can expect your spiritual director to emphasize learning through participation rather than by teaching. Join in on the goings-on of the Benedictines, who meet for prayer in the chapel four times daily and once for mass. Those who come for private retreats (when no program is scheduled) learn solely by involvement in monastic life, and by taking time between scheduled activities for reflective thoughts, prayer, or walks along one of the many hiking trails.

If you're interested but hesitant, consider beginning with a Monastic Weekend; offerings include programs dedicated to religious art, sacred dance, and nature adventures into the New Mexican landscape.

**Season**   Closed to retreatants six weeks out of the year (around holidays).

**Environs**   Adobe buildings on nine hundred acres in the Pecos River Valley. Surrounded by the thirteen thousand-foot Sangre de Cristo Mountains, about twenty-five miles from Santa Fe.

**Accommodations**   Typically double and triple rooms; meals are served family-style at tables of eight. For guests seeking more solitude, four new hermitages accommodate stays as short as a few days and as long as a month (each hermitage unit has its own sitting area, desk, cooking area, and picture windows opening onto canyon vistas). Bring warm clothing, hiking shoes, a Bible, and an alarm clock, and remember to dress appropriately for a monastic environment.

**Activities and Services**   Private and directed retreats for men, women, couples, and families.

**Religious Affiliation**   Benedictine, part of the Olivetan Congregation of Siena, Italy.

**Rates**   The suggested donation for directed and nondirected retreats is $40 per day ($45 for hermitage), with an additional free-will offering suggested for a directed retreat.

**For More Information**   Reservations Office, Pecos Benedictine Abbey, Pecos, N.M. 87552; phone (505) 757-6415 Monday to Friday 9–11:45 A.M. and 1–3 P.M. mountain time; fax (505) 757-2285; e-mail: guestmaster@juno.com; Website: www.pecosabbey.org.

---

## PRAYER AND THE RELIGIOUS MONASTIC RETREAT

Monasteries are popular nowadays as places to get some hard-earned rest, periods of silence, and time for personal reflection. Some say we're turning back to religion at the onset of a new millennium. Others say we've always been spiritual creatures but are finally looking toward the religious traditions of our own culture rather than those of the East or Native Americans. Many pastors and rabbis have said that the public's very turn away from traditional religion for their soul searching has inspired institutional religions to forge ahead with new and enriching pathways in spirituality.

Contemplative practices like centering prayer (which employs *lectio ∂ivino* and an unspoken sacred word), Christian Meditation (the John Main method), the Jesus prayer (also known as Prayer of the Heart), and the Practice of the Presence of God are all relatively new, or newly revived, mechanisms for countering the age-old problem of hunger for meaning in life. Some involve mantras and controlled breaths, combining practices of Buddhism and the Eastern Orthodox Church with ancient Christian methods of prayer, while others revive the work of Medieval and Renaissance European mystics. All contemplative methods can pose personal challenges. Christians today feeling unrest, confusion, or blockage in their spiritual quests are more readily seeking help from trained spiritual directors. Others look to spiritual companionship in the form of prayer groups and group retreats. Interfaith ministries are also on the rise.

According to a 1993 Gallup poll commissioned by *Life* magazine, 90 percent of American adults say they pray regularly. They do so in the form of spontaneous pleas, formal recitations, and attempts at conversation as well as more disciplined forms of contemplation. What binds their prayers is a search for intimacy with the Divine. Since many monastic communities build their entire day around periods of prayer, it's not surprising that people are turning to them for spiritual direction. What aspiring retreatants should know is that only monasteries with directed retreat programs focus on attending to the individual. Retreatants who come on their own, without benefit of a scheduled program, should expect to learn by becoming a part of monastic life rather than by counseling or instruction. Even when retreats are supervised, spirituality is something to be experienced rather than taught.

Though receiving guests is a tenet of monastic life, many houses have had to struggle to balance the continuation of their own communities with ever-increasing requests from the public. Reservations are generally needed for monasteries within driving distance of major metropolitan areas, and can

be months in the making. Of the retreat and religious conference centers listed in this book, some have facilities focusing
entirely on the laity, while others remain home to members of
the holy orders. When visiting these monasteries, try to
remember whose house you're in. Guests should observe deco-
rums of behavior and dress; in some houses, they are expected
to participate in all prayer services, group meals, and quiet
times.

## PHOENICIA PATHWORK CENTER
## Phoenicia, New York

Pathwork is a means toward self-knowledge and personal
growth, blending psychological insights with spiritual wisdom.
The Phoenicia Center's philosophy of service is drawn from a
series of 285 lectures prepared from teachings channeled
through and recorded by Eva Pierrakos beginning in 1959.
According to Eva, her teaching source was a spirit entity she
called "the Guide," which spoke to her on issues of self-respon-
sibility, self-knowledge, and self-acceptance. She organized
these sessions with the Guide into a document (called *The
Pathwork*) to allow others to study them and thereby find their
own paths of self-realization and transformation.

  The thrust of Pathwork affirms the human spirit in all its
potential, but the Guide also speaks at length on the "dark"
side of human nature. Considerations of this sort are made not
to elicit fear but to further understand the internal forces that
plague us. By exploring our shadow side, Pathwork aims to
transform it into a force for positive growth. At the very least,
this kind of exercise can promote the release of muscle tension
to create a harmonious flow of energy (not unlike the philo-

sophical traditions of t'ai chi, though very different in practice).

The center offers a variety of weekend, weeklong, and
even yearlong programs. Individuals not participating in programs are also welcome for retreat. If you are serious about
participating, there is an extensive body of printed material
about Pathwork available for consultation.

**Season**   Year-round.

**Environs**   The Catskill Mountains, a few hours from New
York City.

**Accommodations**   Modest rooms; please call for updated
information.

**Activities and Services**   Hiking, walking, swimming, tennis,
organic gardening.

**Religious Affiliation**   None.

**Rates**   Weekend programs cost up to $1,500, one-week pro-
grams up to $3,000.

**For More Information**   Phoenicia Pathwork Center, P.O.
Box 66, Phoenicia, N.Y. 12464; phone (914) 688-2211; fax
(914) 688-2007; Website: www.pathworkny.com.

---

## SEVENOAKS PATHWORK CENTER

This southeastern center also offers workshops and training in
Pathwork, as well as programs on healing, shamanism, meditation, and earth-centered spirituality. *For More Information:*
Sevenoaks Pathwork Center, Route 1, Box 86, Madison, Va.
22727; phone (540) 948-6544; fax (540) 948-3956; e-mail:
sevenoaksp@aol.com; Website: www.pathwork.org.

## THE RAJ
**Fairfield, Iowa**

Vacations at The Raj present a uniquely luxurious introduction to Ayurveda, the science of personal transformation and perfect health. A specialist in this Indian folk medicine of ancient origins, The Raj offers three-, five-, and seven-day in-residence programs designed to restore and revitalize your unique physiology and combat the effects of aging by stirring up the body's own natural rejuvenating abilities.

The Raj is a palace on the prairie. The decor is country French, the meals gourmet vegetarian, and the health and skin treatments truly sumptuous. Most guests are welcomed by Abhyanga, a warm herbal oil massage performed simultaneously by two technicians. Other rejuvenation treatments include herbalized steam treatments, aromatherapy, and sound therapy. As for beauty treatments, the milk and floral waters bath is especially nourishing. And after the skin-care professionals are through buffing, scenting, and soothing your skin, they'll give you the sponges and loofahs and teach you how to use them yourself at home.

Personalized care at The Raj, no matter how lavishly presented its treatments or pleasurable their effects, remains squarely focused on meeting your everyday needs. The process begins even before your stay. All intended guests are interviewed by phone regarding their current health and lifestyle habits. Based on the interview results, Raj doctors send each future guest instructions for a home preparation program designed to begin loosening impurities in the body. Follow these simple changes in diet and daily routine just ten to fourteen days prior to your arrival and you will draw maximum results and comfort from the rejuvenation programs.

On arrival at The Raj, each guest is interviewed again, this time in person by a Yale-trained medical doctor and a consulting *vaidya* (or visiting expert in Maharishi Ayur-Veda from India). These two doctors assess your current mind-body balance and design an individualized program for you to follow — both during the length of your stay and for at least one week after your rejuvenation program has been completed. Once this postprogram week is up, it's time to follow The Raj's take-home prescription for staying healthy: specific foods, exercises, herbal preparations, daily and seasonal routines tailored to continue and expand your new sense of well-being without putting a strain on your lifestyle. As late as five months after your departure, you can expect a call from The Raj to check up on your progress and answer any questions regarding the prescribed at-home program.

**Season**   Year-round.

**Environs**   A palatial retreat amidst the rolling farmlands of southeastern Iowa. Airports are located at Fairfield, Cedar Rapids, or Des Moines, or private planes can land at The Raj's own airstrip.

**Accommodations**   Single and double rooms in a French country-style hotel, or deluxe rooms and suites in two-story private villas.

**Activities and Services**   Ayurvedic medical consultations including pulse diagnosis; Traditional Maharishi Rejuvenation Treatments (panchakarma treatments) including massage, internal cleansing, and Royal Skin Rejuvenation Treatments. Stress management, nutritional and diet counseling. Transcendental meditation instruction available (not included in program costs). Limited indoor exercise equipment (two treadmills, two step machines, two stationary bikes, free weights), trails for walking.

**Religious Affiliation**   None.

**Rates**   All packages include consultations with a doctor and vaidya, daily treatments, informal salon lectures, and all meals (gourmet vegetarian). Rejuvenation Treatment Packages: three-day $1,611, five-day $2,685, and seven-day $3,760 including single-room accommodations. Royal Skin Rejuvenation Treatment Package (one to five days): $597 per day, including single-room accommodations. A five-day private instruction course in transcendental meditation is available as a supplement to any five- or seven-day program for $1,000.

**Note**   Women's treatments should not coincide with the first three days of the menstrual cycle. Refunds will not be provided if this occurs. Also, treatment is not recommended during pregnancy.

**For More Information**   The Raj, 1734 Jasmine Avenue, Fairfield, Iowa 52556; phone (800) 248-9050 or (515) 472-9580; fax (515) 472-2496; Website: www.theraj.com/raj.html.

## RANCHO LA PUERTA
## Tecate, Baja California, Mexico

Rancho La Puerta began as a summer camp for some very adventuresome adults. In 1940, Edmond and Deborah Szekely, drawn to the powerful and simple beauty of the Baja Peninsula, led a group of friends south of the border to pitch tents and explore physical fitness and good nutrition as a means to healthy living. From the one-room adobe hut that was the Szekelys' first home at Rancho La Puerta, Edmond Szekely—a Hungarian scholar and pioneer in nutrition, diet, and health—would lecture on pesticide-free gardening and low-fat, low-cholesterol meals, very revolutionary concepts in those days.

Over the last fifty years, a few things have changed. The spa now encompasses over three hundred acres of state-of-the art facilities along with another two thousand seven hundred acres of surrounding hills and valleys. Tent camping is forgone for exquisite haciendas, rancheras, and villas (each with private garden), all at a cost somewhat higher than the original $17.50 per week. While Rancho La Puerta has moved up about ten thousand notches on the luxury scale, though, its core commitment to healthy, simple living is unchanged.

Many of the staff are second generation, now serving guests at a ratio of almost 2:1. Such truly personalized service makes for a very productive vacation schedule. From a range of more than sixty fitness classes and spa treatments scheduled on the hour every hour from six in the morning to night, guests can take on as much as they like. Free to plan their own days, they can also take advantage of a personal consultant to help in the decision making. A good consultant will make sure that for the sake of mental health and relaxation, guests schedule some free time to enjoy being idle; toward this end, the grounds are dotted with quiet places perfect for naps, meditation, or daydreaming. Evenings are given over to social events such as lectures, movies, and discussion groups or time alone in front of the fireplace or stargazing from each room's private garden.

It can be fairly stated that this pioneer fitness spa is also a leader in spa cuisine. La Puerta has had fifty years to perfect a lacto-ovo-vegetarian diet supplemented by fresh fish. Guests and world-class chefs alike applaud its tasteful creations, while the eco-minded can get excited about the fact that all produce is organic and grown nearby at Rancho Tres Estrellas, a subsidiary of La Puerta.

The minimum stay at Rancho La Puerta is seven days. Guests arrive and leave on Saturdays; this schedule allows the ranch to increase the intensity of its exercise classes and treatments incrementally until the week is out. Beginning and ending their stays together also encourages guests to form bonds of friendship that enhance their overall wellness experience.

Some guests, however, arrive at this destination for reasons that transcend the modern spa experience: The resort sits at the foot of Mount Kuchumma, considered sacred as one of only fourteen energy vortex points on earth. With or without vigorous exercise, this is a place where spirits can come alive, and the whirling distractions of everyday live become no match for the centering forces of your core being. The spa grounds are the valley acres connecting ocean and desert, which naturally formed a center of trade and spirituality for Native Mexicans. In its truest translation, Rancho La Puerta means "open door ranch." It is a portal onto self-knowledge and strength, a chance to find balance between your outer and innermost manifestations of health.

The energetic magic of Rancho La Puerta can stretch a long way. It certainly has for owner Deborah Szekely, who with her Midas touch founded La Puerto's famous sister, the Golden Door in Escondido, California, in 1958.

**Season**   Year-round. The regular season is from mid-September to mid-June; summer (off-peak) season is from mid-June to mid-September.

**Environs**   At the base of Mount Kuchumma near the southwesternmost corner of the United States, the spa is a short drive through the Tecate Mexican Border Gate in Baja California. Transit time to San Diego International Airport is about three hours.

**Accommodations**   Luxury rooms in Spanish Colonial-style buildings. Each guest unit is unique, with its own garden, and many have fireplaces.

**Activities and Services**   Six tennis courts, volleyball, six aerobic gyms, weight-training facility, three swimming pools, five whirlpool-jet therapy pools, three saunas. Full range of fitness and spa treatments. Extensive hiking and walking trails on and surrounding the spa grounds. Because of the temperate climate, the gyms have sliding glass on three sides to allow indoor-outdoor workouts. Men and women have separate health centers for treatments and massage with private tubs, saunas, and steam rooms.

**Religious Affiliation**   None.

**Rates**   Regular rates range from $2,055 to $2,580 (per week, single). Summer rates are from $1,805 to $2,220 (per week, single). This includes all classes, activities, and meals; spa treatments are extra. All prices are in US dollars, although Mexican tax applies to all room rates, treatments, and extra services.

**For More Information** Rancho La Puerta, P.O. Box 463057, Escondido, Calif. 92046; phone (800) 443-7565 or (760) 744-4222; fax (760) 744-5007; Website: www.rancholapuerta.com

---

## SUNDOOR FOUNDATION FOR TRANSPERSONAL EDUCATION
### Twain Harte, California

Sundoor teaches you to walk on fire. No kidding. Peggy Dylan has been leading dynamic weekend workshops and eight-day training sessions on the ancient art of firewalking since 1982 and founded Sundoor in 1984. What is the purpose of these seminars? To ignite peak performance. If you think it sounds too off the wall, read on. Leading-edge corporations ranging from Microsoft to Re/Max Real Estate and U-Haul International have stoked fires under their executives here. The motivational and leadership skills their employees acquired at Sundoor are applicable to anyone who wants more out of life.

Firewalking has no known origin. Cultures of Africa, Asia, Argentina, and ancient America have walked on fire as a rite of purification, healing, or proof of faith in an ethereal power. Firewalking at Sundoor is also passionate, but practical. Instructions are focused on teaching you to allow that inner fire of yours to burn hot. Walking on coals is only a preparatory exercise for your new life. Witness how, as firewalkers state, when the energy in your body is boiling as hot as fire, you can't get burned. Then learn how this ignitable spirit of yours can inspire, purify, heal, and guide you at work, at play, in relationships, and throughout all other areas of life.

Step off the coals at a Sundoor seminar and you can avail yourself of a number of other activities to promote health, increase self-confidence, and improve relationships. Conscious breathwork is another means to help you tap into your inner fires of spirit—those hidden reservoirs of strength and transformation known alternately as chi, prana, ki, or life force. During another activity, you can learn how to access that strength to break bricks or bend steel with your bare hands.

Seminars are held year-round in San Francisco, other California cities, and (by request) across the United States. Some firewalking adventures operate in France or Peru. Sundoor also offers intensives in breathwork (no firewalking).

**Season**    Seminars are scheduled year-round and the request of groups and corporations.

**Environs**    Seminars travel throughout the United States and abroad (including France and Peru).

**Accommodations**    Hotels, most market price for the area.

**Activities and Services**    Firewalking, lectures, conscious breathing exercises, some martial arts.

**Religious Affiliation**    None.

**Rates**    The cornerstone weeklong Fire Initiation Training Program runs $995, including the training fee and all course materials. (The cost of room and food are additional, and vary per location.) For the ten-day Spirit Walk, or Initiation Level II, offered at the Sundoor Center in France, the tuition is $750, including accommodations and meals. Call for rates in Peru.

**For More Information**    Sundoor, P.O. Box 669, Twain Harte, Calif. 95383; phone (800) 755-1701 or (209) 928-1700; fax (209) 928-4800; Website: www.sundoor.com.

---

## What Is T'ai Chi?

T'ai chi (or t'ai chi ch'uan) is an ancient Chinese martial art and meditation exercise known for its slow, captivating movements verging on dance. Translated word for word from the Chinese, the term *t'ai chi* encompasses *Tao* ("the way"), the route to harmonizing with nature and the universe; *chi* ("internal energy"); and *chuan* (boxing), which can be a real or figurative means of self-defense against life blows by external forces. Put them all together and you've got a discipline for raising awareness, cultivating energy, and exercising powers from within.

The movements of t'ai chi aim to bring the body, mind, and spirit into simultaneous action while stretching and toning the body's muscles. Because it combines meditation with action, even very uptight or out-of-shape people can use t'ai chi as an opportunity to relax and strengthen their bodies without risk of strain. Practiced regularly, t'ai chi can aid recovery from stress-related problems, particularly from systemic problems like rheumatism or structural problems like back pains or knee injuries. It improves posture, muscle control, and flexibility. A recent study funded by the National Institutes of Health found that senior citizens practicing t'ai chi experience fewer falls. Why? Because in addition to its physical benefits, t'ai chi teaches us to pay close attention to our bodies; this attention will tell us what we can or cannot do.

T'ai chi also promotes mental health. Everyone who's stressed out can tell you that the one thing guaranteed to make them more stressed is the constant pressure they're under to relax. T'ai chi doesn't ask for the impossible. It doesn't require you to lie still, and in fact asks you to pay attention to your anxieties as a life force you can use to positive ends. Beginners typically start with condensed breathing exercises that aim to draw energy into the body. Next they learn to store this energy, and then to circulate it by assuming postures and choreographed movements. Finally, this energy can be projected at will to create positive life changes. When it's all over and you find yourself feeling tense again, t'ai chi will have taught you to locate where you hold your tension so that you can more readily release it. The goal is always a relaxed body and mind, and the ability to do more at any moment in time.

---

## TAI CHI FARM
## Warwick, New York

The teachings at Tai Chi Farm are the legacy of its founder, Master Jou Tsung Hwa. Less than two hours from New York, the farm is surprisingly far from the amenities of modern society. Guests opt for a cot in a cabin or a campsite, and there is no electricity or running water (yes, that means outhouses!).

Classes cover the fundamentals of t'ai chi postures and meditation, and include specialized forms of the discipline such as San Shou. Try the exercise Swimming Dragon Chi Kung, a muscle and organ toner aptly named for the way it makes your body seem to flow like a swimming dragon, or Dragon Breath Energy, an exercise that will teach you to use your feelings of stress as fuel for self-discovery.

**Season**  May to October.

**Environs**  Warwick, New York, has a real country feel; the rustic farm setting suits the landscape well.

**Accommodations**  Primitive, no electricity or running water. Ten cabins, each with cots or mattresses for two to ten people (bring your own bedding), and campsites are available. Participants prepare their own meals.

**Activities and Services**  Individual and group t'ai chi instruction; some exercise facilities; swimming in the campus pond.

**Religious Affiliation** No official affiliation, but t'ai chi is based on Taoist principles.

**Rates** Inexpensive. Weekend workshops average $125 for tuition and cabin lodging, while five-day workshops cost approximately $170 for the same. Camp, and the price will be even lower.

**For More Information** Tai Chi Farm, Box 828, Warwick, N.Y. 10990; phone (914) 986-9233; e-mail: tcf@worldwide.net.

## T'AI CHI SCHOOL OF PHILOSOPHY AND ART
**Bellingham, Washington**

Master T. Y. Pang conducts many retreats and summer camps in the Pacific and western United States, as well as around the world. His teachings focus on t'ai chi but can incorporate other Chinese meditative practices. Programs vary in length from three to seven days, and extracurricular acivities usually include nature walks and swimming in lakes.

**Season** Summers only.

**Environs** Programs are typically held in natural, wooded settings at state parks or low-cost retreat centers.

**Accommodations** These vary in type and price according to the retreat site; cabins are shared. Vegetarian meals are usually included.

**Activities and Services** Individual and group t'ai chi instruction; some exercise facilities; swimming in the campus pond.

**Religious Affiliation** None, though Taoist principles are at the heart of all retreats.

**Rates** 3-day programs average $285, 7-days $730.

**For More Information** T'ai Chi School of Philosophy and Art, Box 2424, Bellingham, Wash. 98227; phone (360) 676-8356; e-mail taichi@pacificrim.net.

---

## T'AI CHI IN PARADISE RETREATS
## Hawaii and Costa Rica

What better place to learn to breathe like a dragon than at Hawaii Volcanoes National Park? Teachers from the Pacific School of T'ai Chi in Solana Beach, California, lead five-day summer retreat programs there and in other Edenic locations ranging from rain forest lodges and tropical fruit plantations in Costa Rica to hot springs and snow-covered mountains. Classes are for beginning as well as more advanced students, regardless of age or physical shape. Topics include Balance and Inner Power and Push Hands—a two-person method of t'ai chi for managing conflict and fostering relationship skills.

**Season**    There are summer and winter retreats.

**Environs**    Settings for retreats have included Hawaii Volcanoes National Park, Puerto Viejo in Costa Rica, and Stewart Hot Springs in California.

**Accommodations**    Double-occupancy rooms; three meals per day are included.

**Activities and Services**    T'ai chi instruction; saunas and hot tub relaxation between sessions. Informal trips to natural steam baths in volcanic vents, recent lava flows, black sand beaches, and seaside warm springs. Skiing available during winter Lake Tahoe retreats.

**Religious Affiliation**    None, though the discipline of t'ai chi is based on Taoist philosophical principles.

**For More Information**    Pacific School of T'ai Chi/T'ai Chi in Paradise, P.O. Box 962, Solana Beach, Calif. 92075; phone (619) 259-1396; e-mail: paradise@tai-chi.org; Website: www.tai-chi.org.

## VESTA CENTER FOR WHOLENESS AND HEALTH SPA
## Nashotah, Wisconsin

This Victorian home convenient to, yet a world away from, downtown Milwaukee offers individualized classes and retreats focusing on holistic health and spiritual revitalization. Guests take the first step in enacting new lifestyle choices by designing their own programs from a menu of offerings, with the help of a staff knowledgeable about which spa services, classes, and activities best promote their individual goals. The time frame for retreat at Vesta is generally four to seven days, with rejuvenation and healing packages focusing on stress reduction, nutritional ways to wellness, and cellular exercise. Of special mention is Healing Your Heart, a six-day, physician-supervised program for reversing heart disease designed by Dean Ornish, M.D.

Vesta founder Peig Myota is an energy worker with thirty years of clinical experience in nursing and psychology and specialty training in intuitive-diagnosis medicine. Her Diagnostic Reading Sessions read blockages occurring in the energy body related to a particular physical, mental, emotional, or spiritual injury causing discomfort and illness. Reading sessions are instructional as well as healing, teaching visualization exercises or other modalities for self-care at home.

More generally, however, Myota's expertise infuses Vesta's range of classes and spa treatments with a fresh and interesting perspective. Nutritional courses teach all that you'd expect as well as how certain types of foods and applied kinesiology (taught at press time by a chiropractor versed in Chi Energy Massage) can effectively restore balance to the body's energy system. Relaxation therapies with oils and massage are sensuous spa treats that also demonstrate a full understanding of the generative powers of healing touch. Modalities such as craniosacral therapy (gentle touch to the head and spinal column) work specifically on the body's nervous and electrical systems, while reiki targets the body's major organs and energy centers.

Traditional fitness, yoga, and t'ai chi classes are offered weekly only, so out-of-town guests may want to schedule time for some one-on-one instruction. As for traditional spa services, Vesta knows the value of pampering and beauty treatments; its salon offers everything from facials to makeup consultations and pedicures.

What Vesta does not offer are overnight accommodations. Not unlike other centers focused on wellness rather than the resort business (such as the Chopra Center for Well Being in La Jolla, Calfornia), at Vesta participants stay at local hotels, motels, or inns and are responsible for their own dinners (lunch is served at the center, and most local housing includes breakfast).

**Season**   Year-round.

**Environs**   The center is housed in a historic Victorian house convenient to wooded acres and to downtown Milwaukee.

**Accommodations**   Off-site lodging and meals, with the exception of lunch, which is provided as part of program fees.

**Activities and Services**   Full-service spa with reiki, nutritional and detoxification programs, fitness classes, stress-management workshops (relaxation and deep breathing exercises), diagnostic readings (intuitive medicine). Also, Dr. Dean Ornish's Healing Your Heart Program.

**Religious Affiliation**   None.

**Rates**   Programs average $225 (four days), with many spa services à la carte. Physical evaluations, nutritional consultations, and stress-management consultations (with a registered nurse) are available for reasonable fees. Area lodging ranges from $48 to $145 per night; choose from budget motels or two local bed-and-breakfasts with rooms featuring private bath and Jacuzzi.

**For More Information**   Vesta, P.O. Box 83, Nashotah, Wis. 53058; phone (414) 369-0700; fax (414) 369-0589; Website: www.vestacenter.com.

# PART THREE

# WATER

*Apiaries of my dreams, have you
stopped your labors? Has the
water wheel of thought run dry, do
its empty buckets keep whirling,
whirling, shadow filled?*
—ANTONIO MACHADO (1875–1939)

# WATER

◆

W ater cleanses. Whether an oasis in the desert or a cool shower after a hard workout, water is what we seek to wash away what ails us and start again fresh. It's a natural impulse. We began life buoyed in the waters of our mothers' wombs; as adults, water accounts for 70 percent of our body mass. We need water inside and out—to sustain life, but also to feel alive.

Cold water boosts vigor, adds energy, tones muscle, and aids in digestion. Hot water alleviates pain, relieves internal congestion, releases toxins through perspiration, relaxes the body, and relieves psychic tension. Use both hot and cold water alternately and their repeated stimulating-then-calming effects can actually restore normal blood circulation. Nature's best conductor of electricity, water may also be a conduit to our own healing energies. Sure, Ponce de León's search for a fountain of youth may have been a flight of fancy, but the longing behind it was real enough. The dream of a magical wellspring is, in essence, the need for self-renewal.

Our own fountainheads, however, can be hard to find when we're surrounded by everyday water sources that are chlorinated, fluorinated, obsessively filtered, and, sadly, polluted. Unlike any ordinary seaside trip, the following vacations will take you to purer waters. Spa treatments such as mineral springs, jet-stream massages, and the ancient Greek art of thalassotherapy (treatments using seawater) each use the intrinsic properties of water to cleanse and reinvigorate the body. Dreamwork uses the sight, sounds, and feel of moving water to elicit free-flowing emotions. Creativity workshops, too, make us more buoyant and more willing to tap the source of our childlike sense of joy and wonder. Native American sweat lodge ceremonies, whose steamy dens vividly recall the womb, are perhaps the best example of how water (here in the form of steam) can infiltrate our innermost selves to bring about cleansing, soul sharing, and renewal.

Is a water vacation for you? If you're feeling burned out, physically exhausted, emotionally frozen, or can't sleep, then perhaps it is. These water vacations offer the rush of experience that so many of us crave. They relieve us of those agitative longings that the Buddhists call thirst. For the spiritually curious unversed in mainstream religious practices or New Age transcendentalism, a water vacation is more than rejuvenating. Like baptism, it is a great beginning to a new spiritual quest.

---

## AESCULAPIA WILDERNESS HEALING RETREAT
## Wilderville, Oregon

This rustic wilderness sanctuary provides dream journeys, on land and on water. Named for the ancient Greek schools of dream healing, Aesculapia's programs blend techniques of modern and folk medicine, from neurobiology and psychology to shamanism and its visionary processes. Called Creative Consciousness Healing, this method of exploring your dreams can change how you live your life at the deepest levels of perception. The goal is to tap into your dreams and imagination as energy sources and to ease their flow, restoring a sense of peace and balance that can enhance creativity and move you through times of crises.

Dream journeying is a highly private pursuit, and the personal attention of staff is a must. The number of guests at Aesculapia is therefore limited; there may be as few as three. Daily nature hikes, natural foods, and meditation also prove nurturing to guests undergoing this unique retreat experience.

The highlight of this trip, however, is the River of Dreams Journey. Combining action-packed outdoor adventure with the more spiritual realm of a dream or vision quest, this rafting trip (led by retreat founder Graywolf Swinney) takes guests down one of Oregon's majestic white-water rivers. Short-term retreat residents can get a taste of the adventure in milder waters; guests willing to make a longer commitment can go the full distance.

The Wilderness River Quest begins with four days of mental and physical preparation, learning the practical skills of river navigation as well as engaging in sweat lodge ceremonies, meditation, and beginning dreamwork. The actual river trip lasts six days, during which participants discuss their dreams and visions with their mentor and consciousness guide. The journey ends with four more days of preparation, this time to reenter their lives in the world at large.

**Season**   Call for retreat schedule.
**Environs**   Eighty acres of secluded forest on the edge of the Siskiyou Mountains in southwestern Oregon. Air and bus service are available to and from Medford, Oregon, about two hours away.
**Accommodations**   Shared rooms in rustic retreat house, or camping. Vegetarian meals are included, but guests can also opt to prepare their own meals.

**Activities and Services**   Hiking trails, wood-heated sauna, and rafting trips.

**Religious Affiliation**   None.

**Rates**   Retreats cost $550 weekly, $200 for two days; Sanctuary (a vacation without the rafting retreat) $275 weekly, $100 for two days. This includes board, lodging, and use of all facilities.

**For More Information**   Aesculapia Wilderness Healing Retreat, P.O. Box 301, Wilderville, Oreg. 97543; phone (541) 476-0492.

---

## SPA AT THE BROADMOOR
## Colorado Springs, Colorado

The Broadmoor has a tradition of luxury and elegance dating back a century. Formerly a hotel and gambling casino, the resort was added to in 1915 and converted into a luxury destination by the same team of architects that had just completed New York City's Grand Central Station. No sooner was it completed than vacationing presidents, film stars, and foreign dignitaries started shuffling in and out of the Broadmoor's front door.

This resort knows how to take care of its guests—and the spa, which opened in 1994 as part of the golf and tennis complex, is no exception to this tradition of service. Choose from a spa package or an à la carte menu of more than thirty-five different ways to be pampered, relaxed, and cleansed. Clean Rocky Mountain steams are the source for many hydrotherapy treatments and most certainly the inspiration behind the spa's signature Broadmoor Falls, a treatment combining the effects of a multiple-head Swiss shower with a pressurized stream of conducted water (called a Scotch Spray) for the ultimate in sensations that will stimulate your every muscle into just letting go and going limp.

**Season**   Year-round. The high season is from mid-May to mid-September.

**Environs**   The spa is within a large resort at the base of the Colorado Rockies, just outside Colorado Springs.

**Accommodations**   Luxury resort-hotel accommodations; more than seven hundred rooms and suites.

**Activities and Services**   Aerobics, aquafitness, aromatherapy, body composition analyses, body polishes, aerobic boxing, hydrotherapy, facials, mud baths, body wraps, mud wraps, Swedish massage, shiatsu, sauna, steam room, salt glows, loofah treatments, waxing.

**Religious Affiliation**   None.

**Rates**   High-season room rates range from $280 to $425 per person per night (single and double); Low-season rates from $170 to $315. Check for seasonal spa packages; otherwise services are à la carte.

**For More Information**   The Spa at the Broadmoor, P.O. Box 1439, Colorado Springs, Colo. 80901; phone (800) 634-7711; Website: www.broadmoor.com.

---

## CENTER FOR CREATIVE CONSCIOUSNESS (Formerly New England Art Therapy Institute) Sunderland, Massachusetts

The center's core program, Gateways to Creativity, is a week-long workshop that uses art and other forms of creative expression as a catalyst for personal growth. Participants begin each morning with Sivananda, a gentle form of yoga taught by an instructor who can help you locate interior sources of strength useful in the day ahead. If the theme of that day is removing obstacles, for instance, guests learn the warrior yoga posture. Holding certain physical poses helps us to be comfortable with target senses and feelings, and helps us more fully embody our creative forces.

Daily creative activities can include writing, but tend to focus more on visual means of expression. Guests paint pictures, make masks, or sculpt with clay. The theory is that if we step inside ourselves to bring images from the unconscious to light, the images themselves can become agents of transformation. In short, through creative expression the soul heals itself.

No talent is required, though many guests leave thinking that they possess far more of this than previously imagined. All programs are led by professional therapists with graduate training in psychology and expertise in art expression. Opening doors to playfulness and creativity is fun, yet can also be productive in terms of some very serious goals. Art therapy and other forms of creative expression can help you tap into your creative process, clarifying how you make your life choices. They can increase your self-esteem and consequently enhance your relationships, your career, and even your health.

**Season**   Gateways to Creativity is offered annually each summer; weekend and evening workshops are held throughout the year. Vacation programs are also scheduled for abroad (for 1999 in Oaxaca, Mexico).

**Environs**   A scenic spot in western Massachusetts, about two hours west of Boston and three hours north of New York City. Weeklong intensives take place on the campus of a private girls' school just outside Greenfield, with open green areas and rolling hills.

**Accommodations**   Single dorm accommodations in a nearby

private school, with shared baths; meals are provided (vegetarian options available).

**Activities and Services**   Sivananda yoga, writing, painting, drawing, sculpting, maskmaking.

**Religious Affiliation**   None.

**Rates**   Gateways to Creativity costs $1,300 ($50 late-registration fee).

**For More Information**   Center for Creative Consciousness, 216 South Silver Lane, Sunderland, Mass. 01375; phone (413) 665-4880; e-mail: ccc@2create.org; Website: www.2create.org.

---

## CLARE'S WELL
### Annandale, Minnesota

At the tenth anniversary of this forty-acre spirituality farm, the Franciscan sisters and their guests joined in singing: "Come and gather at the well. Come and gather water. Hear the stories that we tell. Come and gather water." By water they meant Life Source, or more precisely, how we can live in relationship to our Life Source—which refreshes, cleanses, and heals us, and opens our hearts to communicate with others.

Retreatants who come to Clare's Well don't have to be regulars at Sunday services or even Catholic for that matter. They must, however, have a longing for peace and contentment and a sense that these can come with a greater awareness of God in their daily lives. Run by the Franciscan Sisters of Little Falls, Clare's Well takes its retreat ministry seriously. Its owners strive to be healers and reconcilers in society, promoting peace and unity within the human family. The sisters clearly state in their dreams of the future that "people will gather here, but we will not be a conference center. Many will find relaxation on Sabbath Pond, but we will not be a resort. We will celebrate with people, but we will not be a restaurant. We will offer massage and other bodywork, but we will not be a spa."

What you *can* expect Clare's Well to be is a peaceful, natural environment for personal reflection and spiritual direction. The sisters share a dynamic kind of spirituality that's ready to reach out to others. Join them in communal prayer and ritual, share with them your hardships and hopes, or simply relax at the retreat they provide. The grounds offer goats in the barn, snapping turtles by the pond, and include a labyrinth and walking paths. Try a massage to experience the possibilities of healing touch, or lounge in the sauna or hot tub. No matter how you choose to spend your time at the sisters' retreat, you can learn from their lifestyle of joyful service of others, simple living, and reverence and concern for the environment.

**Season**   Year-round.

**Environs**   An Upper Midwest farm located sixty miles west of Minneapolis–St. Paul, Minnesota.

**Accommodations**   Single or shared accommodations in the farmhouse or three hermitages.

**Activities and Services**   Personal reflection, study, dream sharing, communal prayer and ritual, sauna, hot tub, massage, labyrinth, walking paths.

**Religious Affiliation**   Sisters of the Order of Saint Francis of Assisi (Roman Catholic).

**Rates**   Accommodations and meals are $40 per day; therapeutic massage (by appointment) is $35. Partial scholarships are available in the case of financial hardship.

**For More Information**   Clare's Well, 13537 47th Street NW, Annandale, Minn. 55302; phone (320) 274-3512; e-mail: clwell@lkdllink.net.

## DORAL RESORT AND SPA
## Miami, Florida

Located on the grounds of the famous Doral golf facility, home of the famed and sometimes feared Blue Monster, Doral Spa is a forty-eight-room resort within a resort. The spa is so self-contained that it has its own dining room, swimming pools, gardens, and walkways. This is luxury in the finest Miami tradition—lots of glitz, excellent service, but not forsaking the mind for all its earthly pleasures.

A Doral spa experience is a balanced combination of activities and instruction that features a wide range of fitness classes, private nutritional counseling for couples with a noted chef, and interesting twists on mind-body fitness such as Middle Eastern dancing classes, hydromassage by waterfall, and one-on-one t'ai chi instruction. Water treatments are a specialty here, from marine seaweed body wraps to body scrubs using thermal water crystals and mud from Hungary.

**Season**  Year-round.
**Environs**  A red-tiled Tuscan-style resort but with a modern Miami mood.
**Accommodations**  Luxury guest suites within the grounds of the Doral Resort.
**Activities and Services**  A full range of spa services with emphasis on fitness, toning, nutrition, and stress reduction. Free shuttles to and from Miami Beach.
**Religious Affiliation**  None.
**Rates**  Spa suites from $425; spa packages from $585 to $2,580; costs vary depending on season and room type and occupancy.

---

**For More Information**   Doral Golf Resort and Spa, 8755 NW 36th Street, Miami, Fla. 33178; phone (800) 331-7768 or (305) 593-6030; fax (305) 591-8266.

---

## FAR AND AWAY ADVENTURES
## Sun Valley, Idaho

If you love the idea of a wilderness adventure but can't imagine a vacation without the safety and comforts of a full-service hotel, Far and Away Adventures is the ultimate answer to your contradictory needs. This company brings the linen tablecloths and fine china along on its four- and six-day guided rafting, kayaking, and boating tours deep into Idaho's River of No Return Wilderness.

Your adventure will begin with a champagne flight, followed by forty miles of rafting. Exert yourself as much or as little as you want, but most likely you'll find yourself swept up in the team paddling effort. Back on shore, a five-star chef waits with appetizers and chilled wine. Who knew campfire food could be so haute? Guests must sleep riverside in tents, but are greeted each morning with warm wash water.

Other special trip features include an initial physical assessment, nightly massages and bodywork, sessions with fitness and relaxation trainers, and the opportunity to devise a take-home fitness plan. Activities include yoga, kinesthetic awareness, fly fishing, and optional river walks along the Idaho Centennial Trail.

In addition to set dates for Idaho (and some for Yellowstone), Far and Away custom adventures are available for the even farther-away locales of Costa Rica, the British Virgin Islands, and the San Juan Islands.

**Season**   Spring to fall.

**Environs**   Remote wild-river locales, usually in Idaho, but adventures are also possible in Yellowstone National Park and on Caribbean islands.

**Accommodations**   Luxury camping.

**Activities and Services**   River wilderness adventures (three different difficulty ratings), massage, bodywork, aerobics, aqua stretching and exercise, haute campfire cuisine.

**Religious Affiliation**   None.

**Rates**   Four-day river trips from $1,125, six-day from $1,450, including all meals, equipment, a personalized duffel bag, personalized fitness assessment, and exercise classes.

**For More Information**   Far and Away Adventures/Middle River Fork Company, P.O. Box 54, Sun Valley, Idaho 83353; phone (800) 232-8588 or (208) 726-2288; e-mail: adventures@far-away.com; Website: www.far-away.com.

---

## FIT FOR LIFE HEALTH RESORT AND SPA
## Pompano Beach, Florida

Designed to enact the life-changing advisories of Harvey Diamond's best-selling book, *Fit for Life*, this no-frills waterfront resort offers all-inclusive programs to shed pounds as well as furrows on the brow. The goal here is learning to cope better through exercise, diet, and meditation. Programs have scheduled arrival and departure dates and group camaraderie is a must, so don't expect intimacy. Guests range from teens to seniors, all gathering for exercise in an oversize gym.

Days begin with an energetic walk on the beach, and usually include sessions of aerobics, water exercise, yoga, and movement classes. For recreation, boating and snorkeling are popular activities. Special courses help those addicted to overeating, caffeine, or nicotine. Opportunities for pampering include facials, massages, herbal wraps, reflexology, seaweed and cellulite wraps, aromatherapy, and neuromuscular massage. Daily health education lectures and classes in vegetarian food preparation are geared to have you continue the Fit for Life program at home so—a word of advice— take a look at the book and talk to your health professional to see if it suits your lifestyle before booking.

**Season**   Year-round.

**Environs**   Housed in the former Royal Atlantic Spa beachside in southern Florida, about thirty-five minutes from the airport at Fort Lauderdale.

**Accommodations**   Recently renovated motel-style rooms in a three-story building with a central court; some have private patio and ocean views.

**Activities and Services**   Aerobics, water aerobics, yoga, meditation. Facilities include tennis courts, Universal gym, free weights, Stairmasters, as well as a Jacuzzi, sauna, and outdoor pool. Boating, scuba, and snorkeling are popular excursions. Spa services are traditional, including massage, reflexology, facials, and beauty treatments.

**Religious Affiliation**   None.

**Rates**   The seven-night Physician-Nurse Package ranges from $942 to $1,650 depending on season and room occupancy; it includes nutritional counseling, full exercise program, relaxation workshops, room, and vegetarian meals, with spa services á la carte. The seven-night program with all of the above and including select spa services ranges from $1,146 to $1,441; offered seasonally (call for more information).

**For More Information**   Fit for Life Spa, 1460 South Ocean Boulevard, Pompano Beach, Fla. 33062; phone (800) 583-3500 or (954) 941-6688; fax (954) 943-1219.

## GRAND WAILEA RESORT HOTEL AND SPA
## Wailea, Maui, Hawaii

Almost every form of water therapy for cleansing, toning, and stress reduction is offered in this gigantic facility on the Big Island. The treatments offered lend the spa a truly international flavor. For something very special, try an international *termé* circuit: hot and cool plunges, a Japanese *goshi-goshi* scrub followed by a dip in a *furo* tub, a pressure-point Swiss shower, and a waterfall massage. A multitude of hot, warm, and cool baths for cleansing and toning use seaweed, mud and clay, mineral salts, various enzymes, and aromatherapy oils.

An experience not to be missed is the Alii Honey Stream Wrap, in which you are scrubbed with sea salt and drizzled with raw honey then wrapped in a sheet to steam the honey off. Spa services like these are sure to leave you weak in the knees from extended pleasure but, for those determined not to miss a workout, racquetball, squash, aerobics, and weight training are also available on the grounds.

**Season**   Year-round.
**Environs**   A large resort on the much-loved and -traveled Big Island of Hawaii.
**Accommodations**   Luxury ocean-view suites in an eight-story tower, all with private lanai and modern bath.
**Activities and Services**   The emphasis is on toning, cleansing, stress reduction, and relaxation though various forms of water therapy, but also offered are aerobics, racquetball, squash, and weight training.
**Religious Affiliation**   None.
**Rates**   Double rooms from $380. Call for promotional spa packages.

**For More Information**   Grand Wailea Resort Hotel and
Spa, 3850 Wailea Alanui Drive, Wailea, Maui, Hawaii 96753;
phone (800) 888-6100 or (808) 875-1234; fax (808) 874-2442.

---

## Gurney's Inn
## Montauk, New York

For more than twenty years, Gurney's Inn has been a true spa
in the European tradition. Affluent New Yorkers once came
here to take the waters, be pampered, and escape the pres-
sures of the big city—but times have changed, and guests now
come for much more than the seawater. Though a virtual
grande dame in the spa industry, its facilities and services in
recent years have become more and more state of the art. The
inn currently employs experts in integrative medicine and
enjoys a loose association with Stoneybrook Hospital's Center
for Complementary and Alternative Medicine. Pampering and
luxury are still a major part of a vacation at Gurney's Inn, but
so are exercise and innovative mind-body therapies.

The key word at Gurney's is thalassotherapy, or treatments using seawater. One of the country's few true seawater
pools is here, as well as a seawater Roman bath. Rooms have
ocean views of the Atlantic, the very source for these treatments (a pump system feeds the pool with heated water from
the ocean). A walk along the one thousand feet of private
beach is also therapeutic, and among the spa's wide variety of
skin and beauty treatments, the Dead Sea salt glow and seaweed body wraps are perennial favorites.

Exercise at Gurney's also makes smart use of the ocean-
front setting. You can work out in the pool, a cutting-edge fitness center with an ocean view, or an exercise studio with a

floating wood floor, a perfect setting for the fluid mind-body-spirit movements of yoga or t'ai chi. Afterward, you can relax those sore muscles in a Russian steam room, a Swiss shower, or a Finnish rock sauna.

Guests can schedule a health fitness profile to recommend short- and long-term health goals, or a musculoskeletal health assessment to focus on the body's possible weak and problem areas to target their exercise and therapies. Spa treatments range from traditional Swedish massage to amma therapy, craniosacral therapy, polarity, reflexology, biofeedback, and Trager bodywork.

**Season**   Year-round.

**Environs**   A resort with one thousand feet of private beachfront nestled among the dunes of Montauk in the oh-so-exclusive Hamptons at the very tip of New York's Long Island (110 miles from Manhattan).

**Accommodations**   Deluxe suites and five private cottages with heavy-oak-beamed ceilings and sunken living rooms decorated in shades of soft beige, mauve, and blue reminiscent of the ocean view outside every window.

**Activities and Services**   Water exercise and other fitness classes, including yoga and t'ai chi. Thalassotherapy, massage (from traditional Swedish and shiatsu to Oriental amma therapy), various mind-body therapies (biofeedback, craniosacral) beauty treatments (from facials and body wraps to nonsurgical facelifts).

**Religious Affiliation**   None.

**Rates**   A wide variety of spa packages is offered, including a three-day/two-night Escape for $795, four-day/three-night Marinotherapy for $1,360, five-day/four-night Pathways to Serenity for $1,788, or Luxury Spa for $2,019; and eight-day/seven-night New Beginnings: Weight Management for $2,720 (includes fitness consultations and a private trainer). All packages include ocean-view room, three gourmet spa meals per day, unlimited classes and lectures, select treatments, 15 percent gratuities, and New York and local sales tax. Extra treatments and services always available á la carte.

**For More Information**   Gurney's Inn, 290 Old Montauk Highway, Montauk, N.Y. 11954; phone (516) 668-2345; fax (516) 668-3699; Website: www.gurneysweb.com.

HARBIN HOT SPRINGS
**Middletown, California**

At Harbin Hot Springs, you not only soak and swim in the good stuff but also shower, brush your teeth with, and even flush toilets with fresh, local mineral water. Pumped at a rate of over thirty-six thousand gallons per day, waters from the site's seven natural springs refresh and rejuvenate each guest inside and out.

Retreats at Harbin are self-directed and essentially entail use of its pools. Kept at different temperatures, the pools are best enjoyed as a series. The experience begins at body temperature (about 97 degrees) with a long, restful soak in the warm pool where signs read, WHISPER PLEASE. Next comes a period of absolute silence with a soak in the enclosed hot pool. At about 112 degrees, the raised temperature can have the effect of burning away any lingering tensions. Finally, take a cold, reinvigorating plunge into a pool at about 60 degrees. When it's over, you can do the series again or return to select pools (the cold one is great for an early-morning dip, and the warm one for stargazing).

Massage complements the series of pools well. Highly trained, highly caring, and certified bodyworkers offer a variety of massage and health service techniques. The fact that Harbin Hot Springs is home to a California-certified School of Shiatsu and Massage should speak to their credentials but, if not, you might want to know that many massage practitioners at Harbin engage in their work with the conviction of a spiritual practice. The place is run as a nonprofit center for rest and renewal by more than 150 resident members of a non-

proselytizing church committed to a ministry of holistic and spiritual health.

Serious intentions lead to innovation. *Watsu*, a very powerful type of water massage listed in the offerings of many spas, was developed and first practiced at Harbin. Short for water shiatsu, Watsu is a style of bodywork during which the participant is gently floated, cradled, moved, massaged, and stretched in a pool of warm water. A more advanced and often underwater variation of Watsu is called Water Dance (participants wear a nose guard). Sequences above and under water change rhythmically in tune with your breathing, while elements of Aikido and rocking dolphin movements blend into a kind of deeply meditative Water Dance.

As for what to wear in and around the pools, clothing is optional. Some guests prefer to swim or sunbathe nude; others wear suits or go only topless. A strict pool etiquette is observed to make all feel safe and welcome in this environment. Indeed, one guest commented that it was while wearing a suit that she felt eyes on her; only after going unclothed did she feel less conspicuous and, within hours, at a wonderful sense of ease. Away from the pools, nudity is less common, and in food-service areas it is forbidden.

Use of the pools and facilities is free to room guests (campers pay a grounds fee). Outside the water, free classes and events are scheduled weekly; check bulletin boards upon arrival. And outside all this, you should also check the fine print. Meals and many health services are offered à la carte here, and without restraint, the bill can add up quick.

**Season** Year-round, but temperatures from December to late March are not optimal for use of outdoor pools.

**Environs** A northern California valley location with woods, meadows, hills, and streams about two hours from the Bay Area or Sacramento. Also nearby are Calistoga spas (about sixteen miles).

**Accommodations** Three pretty retreat houses with rooms ranging from five-bed budget dorms (separate male and female) to basic rooms with shared bath, private half-bath, or private full bath. Campers are welcome, but facilities for them are limited (pit toilets and rustic showers); there are also some RV sites, all without hookups.

**Activities and Services** Swimming and soaking, hiking. Massage (Swedish/Esalen, deep tissue, shiatsu), rebalancing, reflexology, Watsu, hypnotherapy, rebirthing, acupuncture, astrology, and tarot.

**Religious Affiliation** Owned and operated as a nonprofit center by the Heart Consciousness Church.

**Rates**   Dormitories range from $35 to $45 per person per night, basic rooms $50 to $95 ($75 to $150 per couple); the higher quotes are for weekend stays with private bath. Campers should bring their own supplies and tents. Meals are not included in the room rates; you can dine in the restaurant (indoors or poolside) or bring your own food and make free use of the vegetarian kitchen (no meat, poultry, or fish allowed). Massage, Watsu, and other health services are also not included in the room rates; they start from $35 for a half hour, $55 for an hour, $75 for an hour and a half. In addition, one person in your party must purchase a membership, which costs $5 for a one-month trial, $20 for a year.

**For More Information**   Harbin Hot Springs, P.O. Box 782, Middletown, Calif. 95461; phone (707) 987-2477; Website: www.harbin.org.

---

## HIPPOCRATES HEALTH INSTITUTE'S LIFE CHANGE CENTER
### West Palm Beach, Florida

Until you understand the reason behind the name of this spa, you could easily dismiss it as odd and eccentric. It turns out, however, that the name is a good one and especially revealing of the center's serious health mission: revitalization through a comprehensive process of internal cleansing, detoxification, and nutrition.

Several hundred years ago, Hippocrates told his followers, "Let food be your medicine." Forty years ago, Ann Wigmore took this bit of wisdom to heart and founded Hippocrates Institute. Today the message from Hippocrates is that whether we know it or not, we are in a continual process of recovery from issues both mental and physical that limit our ability to grow. Further, our continually deteriorating health is a result of being unable to release ourselves from the shackles of the past. This bondage—in combination with poor diet and lack of exercise—leaves us vulnerable to sickness and under the false impression that we are healthy simply because we are not diagnosed with a disease.

For more than forty years, the Hippocrates Center has fostered the kind of awareness that helps people change their lifestyle before illness can strike. Its model of good health starts with detoxification, a process that flushes out bodily toxins out along with the demons of our past through a combination of exercise and a healthy, internally cleansing diet of enzyme-rich vegetarian foods (called living foods). A primary example of this diet is wheatgrass juice. Prized for its help in washing out the digestive system and enabling the body to utilize nutrients more efficiently, wheatgrass juice is considered so vital to the Hippocrates program that a juice bar on the grounds is open twenty-four hours a day. Other essential elements of Hippocrates programs include nonstressful exercise, massage therapies, and daily lectures. The Jacuzzi, vapor cave, and sea salt pool are popular spa therapies.

Programs are available in one-, two-, and three-week sessions and the list of testimonials to their success in changing people's lives is long and impressive.

**Season**  Year-round.

**Environs**  A thirty-acre subtropical wooded estate in southern Florida.

**Accommodations**  Shared or private rooms; meals are provided.

**Activities and Services**  Weekly massage, blood test, and evaluation; daily lectures and cooking classes, private nutritional counseling, daily aerobic workouts, group therapy sessions. Therapeutic and exercise equipment, sauna, swimming pool, Jacuzzi, vapor cave, sea salt pool, midweek excursions, lifetime follow-up blood tests.

**Religious Affiliation**    None.

**Rates**    Costs vary with room type and length of stay. One-week programs from from $1,650 per week (with roommate) to $3,850 (private bedroom with private bath). All meals, twenty-four-hour wheatgrass juicer, daily lectures, use of all facilities, and one massage per week are included.

**For More Information**    Hippocrates Health Institute, 1443 Palmdale Court, West Palm Beach, Fla. 33411; phone (800) 842-2125 or (561) 471-8876; fax (561) 471-9464; Website: www.hippocratesinst.com.

---

## HOT SPRINGS NATIONAL PARK
## Hot Springs, Arkansas

People have been taking the cure in Hot Springs, Arkansas, for hundreds of years. The local hot springs were known for their restorative powers by the local Indians, Spanish conquistadors, and early-American settlers; in 1832, all forty-seven springs were designated a national health preserve. Tourists have flocked there ever since to soak away their troubles at national park prices. At the Buckstaff Bathhouse, a treatment that includes a thermal bath, whirlpool, massage, body pack, and hydro shower can cost less than $40. The same services in a more exclusive setting would run three figures. Many choose to take the waters while staying at more costly and service-oriented hotels in the area.

Now doctors are quick to agree with what tourists have known for centuries: The waters here are indeed curative, and

Hot Springs makes a fine home for a center for the study of degenerative diseases, which also serves as a rehabilitation facility for patients after surgery.

**Season**   Year-round.
**Environs**   This is an unusual national park in that it's set within the city limits of Hot Springs, Arkansas.
**Accommodations**   The hot mineral springs flow into major hotels and bathhouses around the city, including the Arlington, Hilton, Downtowner, and Majestic. Hot Springs also abounds with guesthouses and camping facilities.
**Activities and Services**   Massages, shower therapy, hot packs, mineral baths. The area also offers hiking, horseback riding, cycling, tennis, and golf.
**Religious Affiliation**   None
**Rates**   These rates vary from pricey to very cheap depending on your choice of accommodations and service.
**For More Information**   Hot Springs National Park, P.O. Box 1860, Hot Springs, Ark. 71902; phone (501) 624-3383.

Hot Springs Convention and Visitors Bureau, Box K, Hot Springs, Ark. 71902; phone (800) 772-2489.

---

## OPTIMUM HEALTH INSTITUTE OF AUSTIN
**Austin, Texas**

Optimum Health Institute is a wellness center committed to good health and long life. Guests come to the institute in Austin and to its sister in San Diego to reenergize and detoxify themselves. Some come to conquer vices such as smoking and overeating, while others are focused on healing themselves after a long period of illness. Whatever their goals, all commit to a strict philosophy of diet for better health. Optimum foods are high in nutrients and inherently cleansing. This means lots of raw vegetables and wheatgrass juice, one of the most densely packed nutrient cocktails of all time.

Techniques for reducing stress and raising self-esteem are an important part of the educational process. Both are necessary to help keep Optimum guests feeling energized and focused on maintaining their new lifestyle. The institute's motto is Forgive and Let Go.

Optimum offers more than thirty food and lifestyle classes along with its therapy and cleansing sessions. Because of the intensity of focus required and the amount of information needed to understand the OHI philosophy, the institute will accept guests for minimum stays of one week.

**Season**   Year-round.
**Environs**   Fourteen wooded acres in the hill country of East Texas.
**Accommodations**   Private and shared rooms.
**Activities and Services**   Lifestyle classes, health and nutritional counseling, deep-grained massage, chiropractic, colon hydrotherapy. Swimming (neither pool nor Jacuzzi contains chemicals), hiking, gardening, food preparation classes.
**Religious Affiliation**   None.
**Rates**   Shared room with shared bath $500 per week; private room with shared bath $600 per week; private room with private bath $700 per week.
**For More Information**   The Optimum Health Institute of Austin, Route 1 Box 339, J. Cedar Road, Cedar Creek, Tex. 78612; phone (512) 303-4817, (512) 332-0106, (800) 993-4325.

The Optimum Health Institute of San Diego, 6970 Central Avenue, Lemon Grove, Calif. 91945; phone (619) 464-3346.

## ORR HOT SPRINGS
## Ukiah, California

From the 1850s to the early 1970s, Orr Hot Springs was owned and operated by descendants of Samuel Orr, a man of pioneering spirit who brought his family across the country in a covered wagon. Looking for gold, Sam instead found life enrichment in his new property's very own sparkling springs.

The bathhouse built in 1863 still stands, but it now holds four private rooms with porcelain Victorian tubs. Guests soak in mineral water at body temperature in the tubs, and then move on to a redwood hot tub seating five or six at a time. An ice-cold plunge into the outdoor pool completes a bathing therapy designed to progress from interior moments of private absorption to the vibrancy and refreshment of the shared outdoors.

"A relaxed and supportive air" best describes Orr Springs. The place is very low tech. No cars are allowed into the complex; guests are provided a cart at the gate to load up their baggage. Hot springs can smell slightly of sulfur, and the place doesn't try to veil its guests from this fact of nature. Set into the hillside, much of the land is shaded and can feel chilly in fall and the early weeks of spring. While wildflowers may thrive in this climate, some bathers need time to adjust.

Part of the charm of Orr Springs is its communal care. Guests drain the porcelain tubs and clean scrub brushes after use. They stay in modest accommodations, usually group lofts or cottages, and prepare their own meals from their own food in one large kitchen (cookware provided). Clothing is optional, and while it's worn in the kitchen and dining areas, it's rarely seen at the bathhouse and pools in summer months.

Visitors to Orr Springs should expect a reflective time away, with nothing to accomplish and no schedules to follow. Bathing, resting, reading, and playing board games are the only activities here. While the landscape is beautiful, the aura of the place encourages short nature walks rather than rigorous hikes. Bodywork is available for an added fee, with massages and treatments focusing on the individual's well-being rather than primping or pampering. Massage therapists can help you to see where you anatomically hold your tension, and recommend ways to maintain health on a daily basis.

**Season**   Open year-round, but best in fall, spring, and summer.
**Environs**   A remote hillside retreat in the mountains west of Ukiah, in northern California.
**Accommodations**   Mostly shared. Rooms, dorms, and a yurt use communal kitchen; group cottages have their own kitchens.
**Activities and Services**   Bathing, swimming, lounging, nature walks. The lodge has board games, piano, and other musical instruments.
**Religious Affiliation**   None.
**Rates**   These range from $30 (camping) to $130 (cottages) per day; call for special midweek rates; meals not provided. Massage and bodywork from $60 per hour.
**For More Information**   Orr Hot Springs, 13201 Orr Springs Road, Ukiah, Calif. 75482; phone (707) 462-6277.

---

## REGENCY HOUSE NATURAL HEALTH SPA
## Hallandale, Florida

The Regency is a full-service beachfront spa with a holistic approach to health and fitness. Its focus is on weight loss, and programs are designed to help you lose pounds through exer-

cise and diet. Toward that end, nutritional counseling is available on site, as are cooking classes and demonstrations. Guests have the option of three vegetarian meals daily or supervised juice fasting. Personal and group fitness training is available, and class schedules change daily. The location would be a travel destination for anyone seeking sun and renewal, and so ocean vistas and free time to enjoy the beach are essential parts of the Regency experience.

**Season**   Year-round.

**Environs**   A beachfront Florida resort on the Atlantic coast about two hours south of Fort Lauderdale and north of Miami.

**Accommodations**   Rooms range from economy (ground level) to court-view standards, studios, and one- and two-bedroom suites.

**Activities and Services**   Private nutritional counseling, juice and water fasting, cooking demonstrations, gym, exercise and aerobic classes, yoga and meditation. Massage therapy, reflexology, sea salt body scrubs, anticellulite treatments, lymphatic drainage, essential oil body wraps, facials, hair and scalp treatments.

**Religious Affiliation**   None.

**Rates**   Eight-day/seven-night spa packages range from $1,095 to $1,395 per person, single occupancy; this includes three meals and two complementary spa services.

**For More Information**   Regency House, 2000 South Ocean Drive, Hallandale, Fla. 33009; phone (954) 454-2220; fax (954) 454-4637; Website: www.regencyhealthspa.com.

---

## SAFETY HARBOR RESORT AND SPA
## Safety Harbor, Florida

Safety Harbor is best known for its natural mineral springs, discovered in 1539 by Spanish explorer Hernando de Soto—who believed them to be the legendary Fountain of Youth. Today these springs serve as the primary water source for Safety Harbor Resort, filling its three swimming pools and flowing from its water coolers, as well as restaurant and guest room faucets. As for the rejuvenation de Soto craved, we can't expect that kind of magic without hard work. So Safety Harbor has created one of the finest aquatic fitness programs in the country, featuring water aerobics, muscular endurance, water strengthening, and water cardiovascular classes.

Though the setting feels more like a luxury hotel than a secluded retreat, spa services do promote both physical and mental wellness. Guests enrolling in fitness packages can take unlimited exercise classes, including sessions of t'ai chi, dance, and energy meditation, but many typical services (hydro baths, nutritional consultations) must be purchased à la carte.

**Season** Year-round.

**Environs** Twenty-two acres on the northwestern coast of Tampa Bay, ten miles east of the Gulf beaches and fifteen minutes from Tampa International Airport. There are serene views of the bay, but you'll have to walk a few blocks to reach the waterfront. Manatees and other wildlife are frequently sighted off nearby pier.

**Accommodations** Single or double rooms in a 192-room resort hotel.

**Activities and Services** Aquatic aerobics and other exercise classes (cardiovascular and weight training equipment), mineral springs hydro bath, sauna, steam room, whirlpools. Activities include yoga, t'ai chi, cycling, tennis (most courts are daylight-only), boxing, ballet, Middle Eastern dance, and evening energy meditation. Spa services (Swedish and shiatsu massage, some aromatherapy), nutritional consultations, and many beauty salon services.

**Religious Affiliation** None.

**Rates** These vary, depending on package, season, and room accommodations. A seven-night/eight-day spa and fitness plan package typically runs $2,329 (single), or $1,764 (double); four-night/five-day $1,349 (single), or $999 (double). Both include room, unlimited fitness classes, daytime tennis, and three meals per day (other packages do not include meal plans).

**For More Information** Safety Harbor Resort and Spa, 105 North Bayshore Drive, Safety Harbor, Fla. 34695; phone (888) 237-8772 or (813) 726-1161; fax (813) 726-4268; e-mail: safety.harbor@ssrc.com; Website: www.southseas.com.

---

## SEA ISLAND SPA AT THE CLOISTER
## Sea Island, Georgia

This Andalusian-style cloister hotel isolated on an island off the coast of Georgia was the dream of an Ohio auto magnate. He hired famed architect Addison Mizner to design it, and President Calvin Coolidge is said to have opened it. Maybe there's some kind of politico magic here, since presidents-to-be ranging from Eisenhower to the honeymooning Bushes have vacationed here. More likely, it's the spiritually empowering setting combined with the vastness of the sea that inspires its visitors to realize their full potential no matter what their vocation.

Sea Island Spa concentrates on luxury and fitness. The facilities are state of the art, the classes and personal fitness training expertly instructed, and the fitness evaluations hospital affiliated. Thalassotherapy is a major attraction, with saltwater treatments ranging from French seaweed masks to salt glowrubs. Outside workouts, loofah scrubs and paraffin waxings, the location has been attracting guests since as far back as 1928. The original 46-room hotel has expanded sixfold over the years into a complex of 262 luxurious rooms and suites. Golf, the power game, is king here, and much of the local landscape is groomed to accommodate the game. The resort's golf learning center is nationally acclaimed. Nature still thrives, however, and guests can enjoy it by embarking on guided marsh walks and turtle expeditions or by horseback riding along the beach.

The real advantage of this type of spa vacation is that while you explore new avenues of mind-body well-being, your more reluctant spouse can engage in typical resort activities — and just maybe try out a treatment or two.

**Season**  Year-round.

**Environs**  Mediterranean cloister-style hotel on Sea Island, with green lawns and Spanish moss dangling from old, gnarly trees. It's located just off the coast of Georgia, only seventy miles south of Savannah and north of Jacksonville, Florida.

**Accommodations**  Spacious single and double rooms and suites overlooking the beach and waterway, or private cottage rentals.

**Activities and Services**  Fitness classes, full-service spa (aromatherapy, seaweed or Moor mud treatments, massage, facials, Swiss shower, reflexology, skin-care and beauty services). Eighteen tennis courts, skeet and trap shooting, horseback riding, sailboarding, deep-sea fishing, swimming, biking, lawn sports, ballroom dancing, extensive nature activities.

**Religious Affiliation**  None.

**Rates**  The four-night exemplary Renaissance of the Senses package ranges from $1,418 to $2,217, and the five-night signature Spa Experience from $1,772 to $2,771. Rates vary with season and room occupancy. All include room, meals, use of all spa facilities, unlimited exercise classes, select spa services, lectures, demonstrations and seminars, and taxes and service charges. Call for information on other packages and rates.

**For More Information**  Sea Island Spa at the Cloister, Sea Island, Ga. 31561; phone (800) 732-4752 or (916) 638-3611; fax (912) 638-5814.

---

## SEASWIM
## Bahamas and Caicos Islands

Rebecca Fitzgerald had a dream, a recurring one. While she spent her days studying graduate psychology at Southwestern

College in Santa Fe, her nights were filled with dreams of spotted dolphins. She later read in a Jungian journal that dolphins were being used in assisted animal therapy for autistic children. Since 1988, Ms. Fitzgerald has led over one thousand vacationers through a similarly healing and transformative experience. She organizes expeditions to the Bahamas, where vacationers can swim with wild dolphins. Specialists in fields such as interspecies telepathy and shared dreaming sometimes accompany the expeditions. In recent years, she has expanded her organization to lead humpback whale expeditions.

Seaswim's vision is based on the medical research of Drs. Candace Pert, Margaret Kenemy, and David Felten, which looks to emotions as the link between the mind and body, and therefore between physical and emotional healing. Jungians and Eastern cultures alike have recognized that the undulating rhythm of dolphins can communicate a reverence for life and, according to Ms. Fitzgerald, "spontaneous healings" have indeed occurred after human encounters with dolphins.

Wild-dolphin swims take place off the island of Bimini. These are land-based operations; guests stay in historic Alice Town, where Ernest Hemingway penned *Islands in the Stream*. Meals are included and prepared by a resident gourmet. Trips to see the dolphins are scheduled daily, but guests are also welcome to sleep in, go to town, or simply lounge along the long white beaches. When the weather is balmy, the dolphins are especially friendly.

Humpback whale swims are oceanbound and take place near the Turks and Caicos Islands. Guests live on a first-class diving vessel and spend a minimum of eight hours per day among the whales. Much more than a whale-watching trip, this is an opportunity to put down your cameras and get into the water with these extraordinary animals.

**Season**   Mostly May to August; seasons are determined by weather and animal migration patterns.

**Environs**   The white beaches and crystal blue waters of the Grand Bahaman and Bimini Ocean areas of the Bahamas.

**Accommodations**   Cottage rooms and a first-class diving vessel.

**Rates**   A six-day dolphin swim costs $1,595; an eight-day humpback whale swim is $2,395; the half-day scuba course (required) is $75.

**Activities**   Dreamwork, animal play, snorkeling, scuba diving, water skiing, and, most of all, swimming.

**Religious Affiliation**   None.

**For More Information**   Seaswim, P.O. Box 8653, Santa Fe, N.M. 87504; phone (505) 466-0579; Website: seaswim@newmexico.com.

---

### FOR MORE DOLPHIN PLAY

Seaswim is a pioneer in the field of dolphin play, but not the only resource available. The following centers and companies offer swimming excursions:

*Lei Aloha Center, Hawaii*   At this healing center on the island of Oahu, rejuvenation and insights are attained through dolphin and human interaction, including swimming with dolphins. Other activities include lightwork, channeling, and reiki. Bed-and-breakfast accommodations are provided at the Dolphin House. For more information, contact the center at P.O. Box 4277, Waianae, Hawaii 96792-1932; phone (808) 696-4414; fax (808) 696-4454; E-mail: Dolphins4U@aol.com; Website: www.pixi.com/~dolphins.

*Dolphinswim Sinai*   These Vienna-based workshops in dolphin-facilitated therapy bring participants to the Sinai, where they can swim with resident dolphin Olin and her baby. For more information, contact Edgar Hoffman and Norbert Trompisch, Hernalserhauptstr. 30/25A, Vienna/1170, Austria.

*Fly With Your Angels: Swim With the Dolphins*   This Washington-based company offers mystical retreat adventures in the waters of Hawaii. Dolphin swims and snorkeling trips are featured, along with opportunities to explore lightwork, meditation, yoga paths, and theosophy. For more information, contact P.O. Box 1122, Mercer Island, Wash. 98040-1122.

---

## SERENITY BY THE SEA RETREAT
## Galiano Island, British Columbia, Canada

From the lulling sounds and expansive vistas of ocean tidal waters to the guest room chairs specially designed for stressed backs, Serenity by the Sea offers much more than relief from the daily grind. While the retreat's scenery entices its guests to take a seat and some time for reflection, its curriculum offers a surprising number of opportunities for creativity and self-discovery.

Attendance is kept low to maintain an air of informality and accessibility to structured workshops. Most typically run three to four days in the spring, summer, and fall. Creativity retreats include Maskmaking for Women; The Playfulness of Painting; Heart, Healing, and Community; and "Have Journal, Will Paddle," an exploration into the depths of mind, spirit, and ocean. The latter is an exemplary offering to mention since, no matter what workshop you choose, you will be provided with a journal upon your arrival to record experiences. Furthermore, all programs strive to integrate the outdoors with your subject matter, thereby encouraging participants to benefit more fully from the natural environment.

You can spend your free time walking along the waterfront or forest paths, listening to the sounds of waterfalls, or soaking in a steaming tub set high on a rocky cliffside. If that's not enough to lure you outside, native eagles, otters, and seals are irresistible in their charm and beauty.

All programs are instructed by Serenity by the Sea's two hosts: Amrit Chidakish and Shera Street. Amrit is an artist, communication specialist, and bodyworker. Shera is a painter, reiki energy healer, and Gestalt practitioner. They each have more than twenty years' experience in leading workshops. And from the comments of recent guests, they haven't lost their touch. One raved, "I went looking for peace and quiet. I found we can become what we imagine. We can be what we dream of."

**Season**   In full operation during spring, summer, and fall. Accommodation and custom programs offered throughout the year.

**Environs**   A forested island in the Canadian Gulf Islands, accessible by ferry from Vancouver (fifty minutes); call 250-386-3431 for ferry information.

**Accommodations**   Shared private cabins or airy, vaulted rooms in the house. Three vegetarian meals per day are provided for program participants.

**Activities and Services**   Hiking and kayaking. Hot tubs, massages, yoga, energy balancing, creativity workshops.

**Religious Affiliation**   None.

**Rates**   Three-day retreat costs U.S. $210; this includes instruction, lodging (shared), and vegetarian meals.

**For More Information**   Serenity by the Sea, 225 Serenity

Lane, R.R. 2, Galiano Island 42-14, Br. C. V0N 1P0, Canada; phone (800) 944-2655; phone/fax (250) 539-2655; e-mail: serenity@gulflands.com; Website: www.serenitybythesea.com.

---

## TWO BUNCH PALMS
### Desert Hot Springs, California

The name conjures up an image of a desert oasis. If you're seeking luxury in solitude, or plan to travel as a couple, then Two Bunch Palms is a haven of serene calm. If you expect to mingle with other guests, be forewarned that privacy is a way of life here. Guests tend to arrive in twos, many take their meals inside their villas, and signs posted at the springs read, PLEASE REFRAIN FROM ABOVE-A-WHISPER TALKING.

This may sound harsh, but once you've seen the landscape you'll understand the natural call for a peaceful atmosphere. A 1907 survey team of the U.S. Army Camel Corps discovered the location and named it for the impressive sight of a tall cluster of twin palms flourishing on the desert horizon. Legend has it that a couple of decades later, Al Capone became entranced by the quiet splendor of the place and made a hideaway of it. He had a stone fortress built with a turret as watchtower (also equipped with wet bar). Request Bungalow 14, a two-bedroom suite, and you'll find the initials A.C. inscribed in a desktop, along with a bullet hole in the mirror. More recent celebrity was brought to the place by Robert Altman, who filmed a scene in *The Player* with its stars languoring in mud baths.

The focal point of Two Bunch Palms is its secluded rock grotto pools. Mineral water from a nearby geothermal spring gushes out at an amazing 148 degrees. Cooled slightly, it then pours out and over a rock waterfall into a grotto framed by

tropical plants and trees. Enriched by minerals, the water is especially rehydrating. The warm green clay for mud baths is dug from a site on the property adjacent to the artesian well. Mud baths rejuvenate the skin by drawing out toxins and exfoliating dead skin cells; the ability of clay to store energy and act as a chemical catalyst may also explain the psychic refreshment that these treatments offer.

Of the many spa services available, all are indulgent. Facials are a specialty here, but worthwhile to your soul as well as your skin are energy work sessions using color, crystals, sound, and prayer (Esoteric or Color Therapy instruction) and the Native American Healing Herb treatment. Two Bunch Palms is also expert at Watsu, a technique of underwater massage incorporating yoga and reflexology, often described as a return to the womb.

**Season** Year-round.

**Environs**    A desert locale not far from Joshua Tree National Park and Palm Springs (shopping, museums). It's also two hours from Los Angeles by car, and two hours from Indio by Amtrak.

**Accommodations**    Guests have their choice of villas or motel-like structures. Villa rooms are spacious three-room suites (bedroom, living room, and kitchen), including a private garden with whirlpool.

**Activities and Services**    Yoga classes, tennis, bicycling, jogging trail. Massage (Swedish, shiatsu, Watsu, and more), aromatherapy, body scrubs and wraps, facials, cabana mud baths, outdoor mineral pool, isolated sun bins (for that overall tan).

**Religious Affiliation**    None.

**Rates**    Low-season rates range from $175 to $570 per night for two people, double occupancy, including a breakfast buffet; high-season from $201 to $656. Sunday-through-Thursday packages begin at $382 per night; Friday and Saturday at $476 per night. Spa services are à la carte.

**For More Information**    Two Bunch Palms, 67425 Two Bunch Parkway, Palms Trail, Desert Hot Springs, Calif. 92240; phone (800) 472-4334 or (619) 329-8791; fax (619) 329-1317; e-mail: whiteowl@twobunchpalms.com; Website: www.twobunchpalms.com.

# PART FOUR

◆

# AIR

*Minds are like parachutes:*
*they only function when open.*
—THOMAS. R. DEWAR

# AIR

◆

Things just feel better in the open air. No matter how basic our actions—bathing, cooking, sleeping, or working—we pursue them with renewed spirit alfresco. Cookouts are just more fun than cooking in, and mountain hikes feel healthier than miles walked on a treadmill. Despite this, air remains a much-overlooked element. We're quick to marvel at the ocean or a sweeping landscape vista, but we inevitably fail to notice the ocean of air that surrounds us at all times; the life force from which we draw two thousand five hundred gallons during the average day.

Like large bodies of water, air flows in eddies and tides. In constant motion, air can move us. Its currents carry feelings of liberty, as well as the particles and energies that enable us to hear, smell, and speak. In a constant crossflow, air also rids us of staleness. It can invigorate us physically, freshen us intellectually or spiritually (think "winds of change"), and even draw us inward into knowledge of ourselves. Yoga, for instance, uses deep breathing to promote relaxation and raise awareness of our bodily processes. Each breath draws in strength and, as aerobics teaches us, builds better health.

Air is also a place to soar. It's the realm of curiosity and of discovery. Bob Dylan once said that the "answer is blowin' in the wind." Whirling dervishes, on the other hand, become like the wind to reach more mystical states approaching divinity. In short, the air above us invites transcendence. As we breathe out the old and breathe in the new, we expel both pollutants and demons.

So go tell it on the cloud-tipped mountain. If you're feeling foggy headed or at a stalemate of some kind, if you're tired all the time or suffer from headaches, if allergies make breathing a chore, the following air vacations can release you. They can also inspire you and bring new ways of thinking and feeling. Hiking, yoga, and aerobics are about air, as are the healing techniques of Holotropic Breathwork, sound therapy, aromatherapy, and even theater.

---

## AMERICAN ACADEMY OF DRAMATIC ARTS
### New York, New York, and Pasadena, California

Robert Redford, Danny DeVito, and Denzel Washington have one thing in common—they each attended the American Academy of Dramatic Arts. If you've ever wondered whether you've got what it takes to make it in Show Business or are just curious about who you are and are willing to discover it through role playing, summer session at the academy is a great place to start.

A vacation longer than most, this is a six-week acting program. Though run by the oldest professional training school in the country, you'll be happy to hear that no one expects you to be an actor or, for that matter, even aspire to be one. Acting training, not unlike other disciplinary exercises such as yoga or meditation, is an exploratory journey full of self-discovery. It requires you to be in your breath, and therefore in a comfortable relationship with yourself. The goal is not to make it to the silver screen, but to free yourself of inhibitions and test your emotional and spiritual limits. It's all about personal growth, realizing your full potential, and, by the way, it's more fun than a week on the Stairmaster. With a newfound vivacity of air and inner strength, you'll also be prepared to explore all that the exciting metropolitan locations of New York and Los Angeles have to offer.

**Season**   July 6 through August 12.
**Environs**   In busy Midtown Manhattan or Pasadena, in southern California.
**Accommodations**   Not included in tuition, but the academy will provide information about places to stay.
**Activities and Services**   Intensive classes in acting, voice and speech, vocal production, and movement.
**Religious Affiliation**   None.
**Rates**   Rates are subject to change, but the six-week program usually runs between $1,000 and $1,500. Check with the location of your choice.
**For More Information**   American Academy of Dramatic Arts, 120 Madison Avenue, New York, N.Y. 10016; phone (212) 686-9244.

American Academy of Dramatic Arts, 2550 Paloma Street, Pasadena, Calif. 91107; phone (818) 798-0777.

---

## ANIMAS VALLEY INSTITUTE
### Durango, Colorado

The Animas Vision Quest is a contemporary play on an ancient wilderness rite of passage. It offers the challenges and joys of a close encounter with nature as well as an encounter with the soul (*anima* in Spanish). Why the connection?

Because, as the brochure states, "The wilderness is the mirror of the soul, just as the soul is our inner wilderness."

The institute is located in a southwestern Colorado valley called El Rio de las Animas Perdidas, Spanish for "river of lost souls." That's significant first because the adventures it offers attract souls groping for greater clarity, purpose, and passion to their life. And second, because a valley filled with detached spirits is the sign of many successful vision quests, the purpose of which is to shed your adolescent identity and gain the independence of spiritual maturity. The practice is based on the idea that our first sense of self develops before the age of fourteen to eighteen and, while this should only be provisional, without some kind of powerful experience to open our hearts and minds many of us will continue in life making only slight adjustments to that kernel of identity.

Vision quests happen over an eleven-day period, eight days of which are spent in the wild. The first five days are preparation for the essence of your quest, a rite of initiation consisting of three days and nights of solitude in the wilderness. During that time of exposure to the forms and forces of nature, you will fast and enact simple ceremonial processes. Next follow three days of reincorporation activities, in which you share with others the benefit of your experience. Finally, participants are readied for Implementation, the last and most important phase of the vision quest, during which you learn to manifest your vision at home and throughout your daily existence.

Vision quests are open to all men and women in good health, ages twenty to eighty, but couples or family members are advised against participating in the same group. A summer youth vision quest caters to ages seventeen to twenty-two. No previous backpacking experience is required (in fact, half of all participants have never before camped or backpacked), but participants must be prepared to carry a forty-five-pound pack three or four miles up and down steep hills. At least two guides accompany each journey (one of each gender). All guides are professional, with credentials ranging from M.D. to licensed psychotherapists and educators (M.A. and Ph.D.).

**Season** Ten- and seven-day programs are scheduled in spring, summer, and fall.

**Environs** During fair-weather months, you can fly to the small airport in Cortez, Colorado. The Albuquerque airport is less expensive and only a three-and-a-half-hour drive from Durango.

**Accommodations** Before and after days in the wilderness, participants stay at Kelly Place, an adobe-style hotel in McElmo Canyon near Cortez, Colorado.

**Activities and Services** Wilderness adventure, backpacking, Native American ceremonies.

**Religious Affiliation** None.

**Rates** An eleven-day/ten-night canyonland vision quest with a guide ranges from $1,165 to $1,315, including four-nights' lodging and eight days in the wilderness. Scholarships, fee reductions, and payment plans are available for those who would otherwise be unable to participate (contact the institute for its financial aid policy).

**For More Information** Animas Valley Institute, 54 Ute Pass Trail, Durango, Colo. 81301; phone (970) 259-0585; fax (970) 259-8884; e-mail: avi@rmi.net; Website: www.animas.org.

---

### ANTELOPE RETREAT AND EDUCATION CENTER
### Savery, Wyoming

Antelope Retreat is a working sheep ranch in the high-desert foothills of the Rockies. It offers two basic kinds of vacations. The first is a seven-day retreat for visitors to focus on the stillness of the landscape while also partaking in the collaborative work of the ranch. During these Work Weeks, visitors join in on the chores, tend to the gardening, and, while they're at it, learn a bit about the importance of their relationship to nature and the importance of relationships in general to their self-esteem.

The second type of vacation is the exploratory retreat. Most of these begin with a sweat lodge ceremony, during which guests are initiated into the community and learn the importance of truth telling in spiritual development. After their souls are cleansed, retreatants can open their minds and hearts to explore Native American–inspired rites of passage such as Wilderness Quests, a Women's Quest, a Sacred Hoop Week, a Wilderness and Survival Skills Week, and a Spiritual Renewal Week.

Antelope Retreat has no spa services to offer, and several of its programs can be emotionally as well as physically challenging. The decision to attend these should not be taken lightly. Participants who have the most to gain from these retreats will feel at a crossroads, ready and willing to receive guidance that may be difficult or even confrontational.

On the lighter side, Antelope retreats include a June Wildflower Week featuring hikes into the desert in full bloom, and a Yoga Week with ample time for rest and relaxation (though the latter has a twenty-four-hour fast option). Guests can also vacation at the ranch without taking part in a vision quest. They can come alone or bring their family. Certain weeks of the year are reserved especially for families.

**Season**   Year-round.
**Environs**   Remote high-desert wilderness retreat nestled in the foothills of the Continental Divide, just minutes from the Medicine Bow National Forest; the nearest town is Savery

(eight miles, population twenty-five). Antelope is two hours from the Red Desert and about five-and-a-half hours from Denver or Salt Lake City.

**Accommodations**   Guests sleep about four per room in the ranch house or yurts; baths are shared.

**Activities and Services**   Ranching, hiking, gardening, skiing.

**Religious Affiliation**   None, but programs are based on Native American spiritual traditions.

**Rates**   Program fees range from $465 to $1,050 per week ($65 to $150 per day), meals included. Scholarships are available (please call).

**For More Information**   Antelope Retreat and Education Center, P.O. Box 156, Savery, Wyo. 82332; phone (888) 268-2732 or (307) 383-2625; e-mail: ohmakasu@anteloperetreat.org; Website: www.anteloperetreat.org.

---

## THE ASPEN CLUB
### Aspen, Colorado

The Aspen Club was initially built as a sports-performance and sports-medicine center and day treatment spa. Combine the incredible beauty and mountain air, not to mention world-class skiing, available in the Colorado Rockies and it's easy to understand why more than one thousand eight hundred celebrities and high-tech workout enthusiasts keep the gymnasium and sports center busy throughout the year. The club took a major step toward becoming a total health and fitness experience when it launched the Center for Well-Being in spring 1998. The center's mission is to change each client's life forever, not just provide a quick fix. Classes and counseling emphasize changes in lifestyle as the road to health and focus on issues of pain management following injuries, women's health, and balanced nutrition in combination with training to maintain flexibility and strength.

**Season**   Year-round.

**Environs**   High in the central Rocky Mountains.

**Accommodations**   There are ninety-one guest rooms and suites; studios; four- and five-bedroom condos; and private homes. Many come with Jacuzzi, fireplace, and deck. All hotel services are available.

**Activities and Services**   Extensive cardio and fitness equipment in the gym. Most indoor and outdoor sports are available, depending on the time of year, including racquet sports, skiing, swimming, golf, horseback riding, cycling, and fencing. Swedish massage, strength and flexibility testing, private trainers, sports medicine, and postinjury therapy.

**Religious Affiliation**   None

**Rates**   A suite costs $75 to $295 per person per day, double occupancy, from April 15 to December 19; December 20 to April 13, it runs $250 to $795.

**For More Information**   The Aspen Club, 1450 Crystal Lake Road, Aspen, Colo. 81611; phone (303) 925-8900.

--------

## ASSISI COMMUNITY CENTER OF THE FRANCISCAN SISTERS OF ROCHESTER
### Rochester, Minnesota

A place to renew the spirit for a little while, this community center grounded in Franciscan hospitality offers sanctuary for meditating on spiritual issues, personal goals, changes in career, or relationship issues at home or at work. The grounds cover a hundred acres of rolling green lawns and apple orchards, with architecturally inspired buildings in limestone and marble.

The Mission Statement of Assisi reads, "Come and See . . ." (John 1:39) and is extended as an invitation to people of all faiths and social conditions. Inside the reflective, healing spaces of the Assisi Community, retreatants can listen to their hearts, to each other, and, as one sister so eloquently describes, "the still, small voice of God within." The center's Solitude Wing or three-season rustic hermitage offer the most opportunities for quiet retreat.

For those who come to reach out to the sisters, Integrative Therapies, a holistic spiritual healing center, offers a variety of services in an environment of serene beauty, safety, acceptance, and confidentiality. Certified spiritual directors and licensed psychotherapists are available by appointment, as are opportunities for massage, touch therapy, reiki, reflexology, ortho-bionomy, and transpersonal body therapy. The healing center also schedules workshops on Centering Prayer and Christian Meditation as well as on the more general topics of humor, journal writing, yoga, stress reduction, Wisdom of the Body, and Touch and Well Being.

**Season**   Year-round.

**Environs**   Convent-style architecture on grounds prettier than most Ivy League campuses.

**Accommodations**   Comfortable rooms with bed, sink, desk, and chair. One small, three-season rustic hermitage; full baths nearby and kitchen open to meet individual nutritional needs.

**Activities and Services**   Quiet retreat, prayer, meditation, spiritual direction, psychotherapy. Holistic healing services including touch therapy, reflexology, reiki. Workshops on topics of spirituality, holistic health, creativity.

**Religious Affiliation**   Franciscan (Roman Catholic), but retreatants of all faiths are welcome.

**Rates**   Integrative therapies range from $40 to $60 per hour (with psychotherapy up to $90 per hour). Call for suggested donations and fees for workshops and retreats.

**For More Information**   Assisi Community Center, 1001 14th Street NW, Box 4900, Rochester, Minn. 55901-2511; phone (507) 289-2180 for Solitude Wing, (507) 280-2191 for Integrative Therapies; e-mail: acomc@aol.com; Website: www.rochesterfranciscan.org.

---

## RETREATS FOR MANY FAITHS

If it's important for you to visit a monastery or Christian retreat center within your own faith, here's a list of destinations with a range of denominational affiliations:

- (Episcopalian) *All Saints Episcopal Convent,* P.O. Box 3127, Catonsville, Md. 21228; phone (410) 747-4104, or St. Gregory's Abbey, 56500 Abbey Road, Three Rivers, MI 49093-9595; phone (616) 244-5893; e-mail guestsga@net-link website www2.inetdirect.net/~dburton/osb/guest.html.

- (Lutheran) *St. Augustine's House,* P.O. Box 125, Oxford, Mich. 48371; phone (810) 628-2604.

- (Mennonite) *The Hermitage,* 11321 Dutch Settlement Road, Three Rivers, Mich. 49093; phone (616) 244-8696.

- (Methodist) *The Florida United Methodist Life Enrichment Center,* P.O. Box 490108, Leesburg, Fla. 34749; phone (352) 787-0313.

- (Presbyterian) *Menucha Retreat and Conference Center,* 38711 East Crown Point Highway, P.O. Box 8, Corbett, Oreg. 97019; phone (513) 695-2243 (see also Ghost Ranch, page 171)

- (Quaker) *Pendle Hill,* 338 Plush Mill Road, Wallingford, Penn. 19086; phone (610) 566-4507 or (800) 742-3150.

- (Russian Orthodox) *Monastery of the Holy Cross,* 19520 Darnestown Road, Beallsville, Md. 20839; phone (310) 349-5834.

- (Ukranian Catholic) *Monastery of Mount Tabor,* P.O. Box 217, 17001 Tomki Road, Redwood Valley, Calif. 95470; phone (707) 485-8959.

---

## BOULDER OUTDOOR SURVIVAL SCHOOL
### Boulder, Utah

If air means freedom, Boulder Outdoor Survival School (BOSS) is a surefire way of achieving it. Participants in this twenty-seven-day adventure in the Utah desert are given a blanket, a poncho, a knife, and a change of clothes. After several days of fitness testing and intensive instruction in getting along without cell phones, refrigeration, and takeout, they are sent out in small groups into the wilderness to test themselves against the elements. Sounds a little like a John Wayne movie, but the BOSS experience is not about playing cowboys and Indians, nor is it about doing yoga under the desert stars. Instead it is a powerful wakeup call to the strength of our survival instincts and the force of our free will. It's closer to real independence than many of us dare to go.

If you're healthy and fit enough to make it through the first two weeks as part of a group, the ultimate payoff is to venture out alone on a three- to five-day Solo/Quest.

To get the most from this incredibly personal experience, BOSS recommends a commitment to the twenty-seven-day adventure. But for those who truly cannot get away for this long, it also offers worthwhile seven- and fourteen-day versions. Incidentally, as "on your own" as you might feel, expert supervision and emergency sustenance are never far away.

**Season**   May through September.
**Environs**   The desert terrain of south-central Utah.

**Accommodations**   A blanket, an army poncho, a knife, a change of clothes, and the great outdoors.

**Activities and Services**   Wilderness treks with minimal equipment and food.

**Religious Affiliation**   None.

**Rates**   The twenty-seven-day Survival School costs $2,425, the fourteen-day $1,395, the seven-day $850.

**For More Information**   Please note that during some months out of the year the contact number for BOSS is in Boulder, Colorado, rather than Boulder, Utah. Contact the appropriate location during these time frames:

From May 1 to September 14; Boulder Outdoor Survival School, P.O. Box 1345, Boulder, Utah 84716; phone (800) 335-1040 or (801) 335-7040.

From September 15 to April 30: Boulder Outdoor Survival School, P.O. Box 1590, Boulder, Colo. 80306; phone (800) 335-7040 or (303) 444-9779; Website: www.boss-inc.com.

---

## COOLFONT RESORT
### Berkeley Springs, West Virginia

Nestled in the foothills of Appalachia, Coolfont Resort is about recreation, relaxation, and cool mountain air. What makes this treetop getaway different from other vacations is that at Coolfont, you can acquire the physical, behavioral, and motivational skills necessary to breathe free in your everyday life.

Coolfont Resort boasts an outstanding six-night smoke-cessation program recognized by the American Lung Association, American Heart Association, and American Cancer Society. The Learn to Break Free From Smoking vacation is a structured experience designed to help you cope with the physical, mental, and emotional processes of becoming a nonsmoker. Stretching and yoga classes, woodland hikes, and swims are among the many activities offered to alleviate the physical discomforts that some people experience while withdrawing from nicotine. Professional massages, facials, and other natural therapeutics also play a part in easing the minds of many guests who, before Coolfont, had repeatedly failed in their efforts to make this vital lifestyle change. While visitors receive much personal attention during their stay, one of the most positive aspects of the Break Free Program is the tremendous group support developed throughout the week.

Vacationing with a nonsmoker? Not to worry—visitors to Coolfont come for traditional spa services and resort activities, as well as for weight loss and stress management. Wellness and fitness classes are offered from morning to night, 365 days a year, and single-theme weekends and weeklong programs are available in areas such as t'ai chi, yoga, Swedish massage, dynamic walking, and herbs for health. Coolfont's one thousand three hundred woodland acres also offer a full range of seasonal sports and activities.

**Season** Year-round.

**Environs** Coolfont is convenient to the Mid-Atlantic region: a two-hour drive from Washington, DC and Baltimore, a three-hour drive from Pittsburgh and Richmond.

**Accommodations** Rooms range from standard accommodations in a manor house or woodland lodge ( each with air-conditioning and private bath) to deluxe suite accommodations in alpine chalets equipped with whirlpool tubs, private decks, woodstoves, and porches for sleeping.

**Rates** The resort charges $72 to $114 per person per night. Break Free charges $1,195 (double occupancy), or $1,395 (single occupancy); this includes accommodations for six days, meals, use of all facilities, program activities, and gratuities.

**Activities and Services**   T'ai chi, yoga, dynamic walking, tennis, hiking, fishing, horseback riding, cross-country skiing, swimming (indoor lap pool), boating, basketball, volleyball, golf (a nearby course designed by Robert Trent Jones is at Capacon State Park). Massages, facials, natural therapeutics, sauna, whirlpool.

**Religious Affiliation**   None.

**For More Information**   Coolfont Resort, Route 1, Box 710, Berkeley Springs, W.V. 25411; phone (800) 888-8768 nationwide, or (304) 258-4500 in West Virginia; e-mail: reserve@coolfont.com; Website: www.coolfont.com.

---

### SEVEN MORE COOL PLACES TO STOP SMOKING

The following spas and resorts also operate celebrated smoke-cessation programs:

- Canyon Ranch, Arizona; phone (520)749-9000 (also see page 6)
- Living Springs Retreat, New York; phone (914) 526-2800
- The Oaks, Ojai, California; phone (805) 646-5573 (also see page 183)
- The Palms, Palm Springs, California; phone (619) 325-1111
- Sans Souci Health Resort, Ohio; phone (937) 848-4851
- Wildwood Lifestyle Center and Hospital, Georgia; phone (706) 820-1490 (also see page 52)

---

### THE COOPER WELLNESS CENTER
### (OF THE COOPER INSTITUTE OF AEROBICS)
### Dallas, Texas

You might not think of going to Dallas to visit a luxury medspa, but if you knew the reputation of Dr. Kenneth

Cooper you might think again. Cooper knows spas, and he knows fitness. A well-respected physician, he wrote the definitive book on aerobics (*Aerobics*); his latest book, *Antioxidant Revolution*, is turning heads and treadmill belts. One of the first to espouse the idea that there are concrete medical benefits to vigorous, well-monitored exercise (especially when linked to a healthy diet), Cooper is now expanding his premier aerobics center into the next millennium of fitness retreats. His prototype medspa, the Cooper Wellness Center, is housed inside the world-renowned Cooper Institute of Aerobics in Dallas. Sharing its state-of-the-art facilities, the new center also builds on the old's mission of cardiovascular health.

Wellness Center programs aim to change the way people eat, how they exercise, and ultimately how they think about themselves. Daily exercise is, of course, required. Guests rise early for days filled with classes, lectures, and consultations. All are carefully monitored by a staff of physicians, nutritionists, and exercise physiologists, who guide them in setting and attaining maximum goals.

A minimum stay of one week (although two weeks is preferred) is recommended to ensure that the seeds of a new lifestyle are firmly planted. But programs of shorter duration are also available. Families are encouraged to be a part of the process, learning about the participant's issues of health and fitness, and how they can help their loved one achieve desired goals.

**Season** Year-round.

**Environs** A campuslike setting about twenty minutes from downtown Dallas.

**Accommodations** The guest lodge at the Wellness Center is a Colonial-style hotel offering single- or double-occupancy rooms. Some alternative lodging is available off campus (center guests receive special rates). Three meals per day, all low in sodium, fat, and cholesterol, are provided.

**Activities and Services**   Fitness and nutritional counseling, individual and group exercise sessions, cooking classes, lectures, full complement of exercise and fitness machines, Swedish massage, yoga. Two heated outdoor pools, four racquetball courts, four tennis courts, basketball, volleyball, jogging paths. Beauty salon on premises.

**Religious Affiliation**   None.

**Rates**   The four-night Premier Program (single) runs $2,592, the six-night Premier Program $3,440, the thirteen-night Premier Program $5,210. Rates include all meals, use of all facilities, exercise sessions, lectures, fitness assessment, stress management, all program workshops, personal training sessions, and all sports and recreational activities.

**For More Information**   The Cooper Wellness Center, 12230 Preston Road, Dallas, Tex. 75230-9967; phone (800) 444-5192 or (972) 386-4777.

---

## THE JEWISH SPIRITUAL RETREAT

Of the large number of baby boomers who came to adolescence in the 1960s or early 1970s seeking spiritual shelter in alternative religions or lifestyles, a great many came home in later years to their Jewish faith. They brought with them new spiritual practices, renewed passions, and their open, inquiring minds. A Jewish renewal movement is in the air of the approaching millennium, and several resources are available for us to capture its spirit.

Retreat houses in the formal sense have not played as large a historical role in the Jewish tradition as they have in Buddhism or Christianity. But the idea of *tikkun nefesh*, Hebrew for healing, repairing, and transforming, lends itself well to retreat. A number of local and nationwide Jewish organizations in the United States offer exploratory workshops and seminars in Jewish meditation. Some focus on reviving ancient Jewish contemplative practices; others bring practices from other traditions, such as guided visualizations, Hatha yoga, or Zen meditation, into harmony with the core of Jewish faith. Many of these retreat opportunities, especially those focusing on the kabala, are frequented by non-Jews attracted to the mystical approach.

More than just rest and renewal, the Jewish meditative retreat is a means to explore the very profound Jewish themes of freedom, peace, and thoughtful action.

---

## ELAT CHAYYIM
## Accord, New York

Hebrew for "the tree of life," Elat Chayyim is a center of Jewish Renewal and healing. Located on thirty-five quiet country acres in the Catskill Mountains, the place serves as both a sanctuary and an adult learning center. It holds week-long summer retreats, creativity workshops, Hebrew immersion courses, singles retreats, and a special Healing Week. Meditative retreats are regularly offered for both the novice and the experienced practitioner. Instruction is provided by a range of visiting faculty, from rabbinic visionaries to Talmudic scholars, respected authors, psychologists, and artists. A typical day could include prebreakfast hikes, yoga, or prayer services. Conscious eating is promoted through attention to organic foods, and by the saying of *brachot* (blessings). A highlight for many are the Friday and Saturday Shabbat services, which fill the air with song and joyful prayer.

**Season**   Year-round.

**Environs**   Located on thirty-five wooded acres in the Catskill Mountains; thirty-five minutes southwest of Woodstock and two hours from New York City and northern New Jersey. Minutes from the Mohonk Preserve and Minnewaska State Park.

**Accommodations**   Single, double, and quadruple rooms with private or shared baths. There's camping space for about thirty guests only; the meals are vegetarian Kosher.

**Activities and Services**   Retreats appealing to the spirit and intellect. Instruction in Jewish meditation and healing traditions. Outdoor pool, indoor hot tub, tennis, volleyball, basketball.

**Religious Affiliation**   Jewish, welcoming secular Jews as well as members of all denominations from Reform to Conservative, Reconstructionist, Post-Modern, and Orthodox.

**Rates**   From $50 to $100 per day, including all programming, food, lodging, and facility costs. Payment plans, work exchange, and limited scholarships are available.

**For More Information**   Elat Chayyim, 99 Mill Hook Road, Accord, N.Y. 12404; phone (800) 398-2630 or (914) 626-2037; e-mail: elatchayyi@aol.com; Website: members.aol.com/elatchayyi.

---

## MORE DESTINATIONS FOR JEWISH SPIRITUAL RETREAT

*Heart of Stillness Retreat Center, Jamestown, Colorado*   A secluded Rocky Mountain retreat center under the direction of Rabbi David Cooper and Shoshana Cooper. Offerings include meditation courses and opportunities for deep listening and silence. P.O. Box 106, Jamestown, Colo. 80455; phone (303) 459-3431.

*LivingWaters, Davie, Florida*   A Jewish spiritual health spa under the direction of Rabbi Shoni Labowitz. Activities include meditation and yoga with a kabbalistic focus. 11450 SW 16th Street, Davie, Fla. 33325; phone (954) 476-7466.

*Rose Mountain Center, Las Vegas, New Mexico*   At eight thousand-feet in the Sangre de Christo Mountains. An isolated location with simple accommodations for rest and renewal; under the direction of Rabbi Shefa Gold and Andy Gold. P.O. Box 355, Las Vegas, N.M. 87701; phone (505) 425-5728.

---

## ESALEN INSTITUTE
## Big Sur, California

The Esalen Institute, a leader in experimental and alternative education, was one of the first of its kind. It was founded in 1962, at a time in history when creative thinkers, artists, and philosophers in the West were beginning to question how we learn and how little we are encouraged to learn about ourselves as individuals. Many hungry souls of the era turned to ancient Eastern philosophies for answers only to become adrift in a sea of knowledge. Ultimately what they sought were practical Western applications of the methods and values that had inspired them among other cultures. Esalen emerged as a place for such trials, where groups attempted to apply new ideas in workshops and seminars aimed at helping individuals see their own capacities for reaching their full potential.

Blending traditions of the East and West, Esalen's offerings are vast and varied. Most focus on topics of mental and spiritual growth. With a teaching staff of more than 150 (all leaders in their respective fields), guests can choose to explore classes on topics relating to the arts, creativity, relationships, professional growth, spiritual and religious studies, dream-work, somatics, and health and healing. If Esalen has a unifying credo, it's one of respect for the human body and spirit, a commitment to refine what constitutes personal sanctuary, and the human possibility of change. If that sounds like psychobabble, it's not. In fact, Esalen brochures clearly note that no psychotherapy is involved, and that the burden of self-realization and transformation lies solely on the individual.

For the first-time visitor, however, some form of help is needed in navigating through Esalen's weighty tome of a catalog. Toward that end, the institute offers a series of overview workshops called Experiencing Esalen, which help newcomers identify what works best for them, and at what pace to proceed. These sampler programs focus on the different approaches a workshop could take, such as Gestalt, massage, sensory awareness, and meditation. Another, less expensive sampling option is Esalen's twenty-eight-day Work Study Program, during which participants learn by sitting in on various workshops and contributing to the community at large.

Visitors to the institute may come away with all kinds of insights, but all leave convinced that there may be no more beautiful place on earth to search for personal awareness and growth. Views of some of the best of California's rugged Pacific coastline offer an inspiring natural backdrop for furthering knowledge of our abilities and life options. Rocks and thrashing waves can be seen and heard from Esalen's walkways, trails, hot springs, and bath.

**Season**   Year-round.
**Environs**   A scenic Pacific coastal retreat south of San Francisco near Monterey.
**Accommodations**   Shared housing (two or more per room); three meals per day are included.

**Activities and Services**   Program areas in the arts, creativity, biofeedback, hypnosis, family relationships, professional growth, spiritual and religious studies, dreamwork, somatics, ecology, health and healing, martial arts, yoga, and fitness sports. Natural hot springs and a pool are found on the property (swimsuit optional).
**Religious Affiliation**   None.
**Rates**   Cost varies per workshop and length of stay. The standard seven-day rate per person is $1,370 (not including workshop or program fees). Some work study and scholarships are available for those seeking a longer commitment to study.
**For More Information**   Esalen Institute, Highway 1, Big Sur, Calif. 93920-9616; phone (408) 667-3000; Website: www.esalen.org.

———————

FEATHERED PIPE RANCH
**Helena, Montana**

Some say that transformative energies are in the air and that all we need is a few crisp lungfuls to get a fresh start on life. Well, the Feathered Pipe Ranch offers invigorating breaths of mountain air and a lot more—from yoga retreats to a variety of personal growth workshops promoting health, happiness, and positive change.

A small Eden set against the tree-covered northern Rockies and surrounded by thousands of acres of Montana forest, the ranch is both rustic and nurturing in unexpected ways. The food is vegetarian gourmet, and the cedar bathhouse sports a sauna, hot tub, and rooms for massage. Visiting faculty are tops in their field but, unlike other premier retreat centers offering a dizzying array of workshops, the Feathered Pipe schedules only one program at time. This eliminates distractions for guests, encourages new friendships, and allows guests to benefit simultaneously from both instruction and environment. In general, a growing intimacy with both nature and spirit is the goal of all programs in this uniquely harmonious setting.

In Native American folklore, it is the feathered pipe that is symbolic of the connection between the circle of life and the Great Spirit. Shamanic wisdom is taught at the Feathered Pipe, but so too are many worldviews of wholeness encouraging work in nutrition, music, the arts, astrology, and bodywork. Programs are typically eight days long, and yoga is a specialty. In fact, a greater variety of yoga styles was taught here in 1999 than at several of the nation's leading ashrams.

For those wanting to travel farther than Montana, the Feathered Pipe also manages one- to two-week tours abroad. Examples include yoga workshops among the ruins at Machu Picchu and on Mexico's Isla Mujeres, as well as a summer journey of Eclipse Chasing in Romania and Turkey with Dr. Andrew Weil.

**Season**    Workshops are offered on site during spring and summer.

**Environs**    Natural log and stone buildings in the heart of the northern Rockies surrounded by miles of forested mountains, a sparkling lake, and abundant wildlife.

**Accommodations**    Rooms are dormitory-style (up to four people per room). Limited semiprivate space is available, or for privacy and a close but not uncomfortable relationship with nature, think about sleeping in a yurt or tepee. Meals are mostly vegetarian and very well liked among ranch guests.

**Activities and Services**    Yoga, natural medicine, music, women's spirituality, and astrology intensives. Occasional river-rafting or horseback-riding excursions. Hot tub, sauna, and massage are available.

**Religious Affiliation**   None.

**Rates**   Typical programs range from $1,195 to $1,765 (with some shorter programs as low as $775); this price includes all instruction, lodging, meals, and general use of facilities. Add $250 for a double room with private bath or $150 for a double room with shared bath. Some scholarships are available, based on financial need.

**For More Information**   Feathered Pipe Ranch, Box 1682, Helena, Mont. 59624; phone (406) 442-8196; fax (406) 442-8110; e-mail: fpranch@initco.net.

---

GHOST RANCH
**Abiquiú, New Mexico**

Ghost Ranch advertises itself as "an open space for the spirit, body and mind." A year-round education and mission center of the Presbyterian Church high in the mountains of northern New Mexico, Ghost Ranch is a self-contained entity covering roughly twenty-one thousand acres of territory. Twenty minutes from the nearest general store in Abiquiú, the location is so remote that phones and faxes are by radio-wave transmission and consistently problematic. A perfect place to rest and recover from damages incurred in our overly hectic and mechanized society, Ghost Ranch offers private retreats and programs that take a spiritually recreational approach to topics as varied as theology, paleontology, Spanish arts and crafts, music, ethics, and social justice and ecology.

The magic of Ghost Ranch is in its setting. Georgia O'Keeffe came here in the 1930s and stayed until her death in 1986. Attracted by the contradictory grandeur and transience of the landscape, she painted animal bones set against an expansive sky and flowers in full bloom on desert ground —

ideal imagery for those questing, or questioning faith. How guests go about this kind of quest depends on their own wants and needs. Summertime is when most seminars happen; these emphasize personal growth through community involvement. From January to May, the ranch is open to spiritual retreatants not participating in programs.

Should guests choose to attend, services of meditation and community worship are held each morning during summer seminars, with all-ranch Eucharist services scheduled for Sundays only. Summer guests can also meet with a chaplain on staff.

**Season**   Summer is peak season. Closed December.

**Environs**   More than twenty thousand acres of high-desert land with towering rock mesas and far-reaching plains; about an hour northwest of Santa Fe, 125 miles south of Albuquerque (nearest airport).

**Accommodations**   Simply furnished rooms: singles, doubles, bunks, adobe casitas (single rooms cannot be guaranteed during peak season); only half are winterized. Two on-site campgrounds. Meals are served cafeteria-style, vegetarians accommodated.

**Activities and Services**   Hiking and observation, educational and art workshops, community worship and prayer. Swimming pool and excellent library on site. Call for biannual Elderhostel programs, and for special college student workshops.

**Religious Affiliation**   Presbyterian Church (U.S.) owned and operated, but the ranch welcomes members of diverse faiths.

**Rates**   From $50 per day plus course price (less than $500); add $20 per night for single accommodations. Some work study is available.

**For More Information** Ghost Ranch, H.C. 77 Box 11, Abiquiú, N.M. 87510; phone (505) 685-4333; fax (505) 695-4519; e-mail: ghostranch@newmexico-ghostranch.org; Website: www.newmexico-ghostranch.org.

---

HEARTWOOD INSTITUTE
**Garberville, California**

Simple and straightforward with few frills, Heartwood is a vocational school for those practicing healing arts such as massage therapy, hypnotherapy, and addiction counseling. Professionals come here year-round for the resources and inspiration to attain higher levels of physical, psychological, and spiritual well-being in their lives and in their work. During scheduled weekends and wellness retreats, guests are welcome to share in this type of learning. You don't have to want to be a professional healer, but you should have some general understanding of a healthy holistic lifestyle and the desire to further your knowledge.

Retreats are packed with classes, bodywork, yoga, meditation, and discussion. Subjects covered include topics for couples and relationships, women's issues, natural healing, and loving communication. Guests may also request to schedule personalized programs of therapeutic treatment and arrange private sessions with Heartwood practitioners.

**Season** Open year-round by appointment; retreats for the public otherwise have fixed start and end dates (call for schedule).
**Environs** The institute is located on two hundred acres of forest- and meadowland on the northern coast of California.

**Accommodations**    A small number of dormitory-style rooms with shared baths and thirty-six campsites.

**Activities and Services**    Yoga, t'ai chi, massage, polarity therapy, hypnotherapy, acupressure, breathwork, transformational therapy, nutritional counseling. Swimming, biking, walking, hiking, hot tub, sauna.

**Religious Affiliation**    None.

**Rates**    Single (per night) $110, double (per night) $90, campsite (per night) $55. Weekend wellness retreats $240 (single), $420 (two people). These rates include all meals.

**For More Information**    Heartwood Institute, 220 Harmony Lane, Garberville, Calif. 95542; phone (707) 923-5000; fax (707) 923-5010; Website: www.heartwoodinstitute.com.

---

## INSIGHT AND OPENING RETREATS
## Forest Knolls, California

Insight and Opening Retreats are designed to open your heart and mind as well as your lungs. Through a combination of Holotropic Breathwork and Buddhist insight meditation (*vissipana*), participants can explore and release the energy within themselves that brings healing. Because most of these intensive weeklong sessions are conducted in silence, guests are initiated by attending classes and lectures that provide an introduction to the process and theory, along with technical instruction in the work itself.

Holotropic Breathwork is a profound method of inner exploration developed by Stan and Christina Grof. Based on modern consciousness research and ancient rituals, it involves working with a partner through sessions of deep breathing, marked by a diversity of music, and moments of focused bodywork and mandala drawing to release energy. Each partner alternates in the roles of sitter and breather, and so both share in and monitor each other's journey of spiritual and emotional cleansing.

Vissipana, or insight meditation, is a simple and accessible training in awareness of the breath and body, used to unlock blockages of the heart and mind. It begins with simple breathing from a sitting position to center thoughts and calm the mind and then continues as cycles of eating, sitting, and walking while maintaining the contemplative state. While its practice holds the promise of healing, a more long-term goal is to live more freely and at peace.

Instructors are qualified professionals holding high degrees in medicine, psychiatry, and clinical psychology and are also well learned in Eastern meditative practices and philosophy. They strongly advise that the intensity of their retreats can place real demands on the body and mind; those with serious health or emotional problems are urged not to participate.

**Season**   Call for schedule and dates.

**Environs**   Varies with each retreat, typically an adult camp or campus atmosphere.

**Accommodations**   Usually dormitory-style, but can change with location of retreat.

**Activities and Services**   Instruction and application of Holotropic Breathwork and Buddhist insight meditation, massage and bodywork, mandala drawing.

**Religious Affiliation**   Buddhist principles are involved, but no formal religious affiliation or instruction.

**Rates**   Rates vary per location but typically range between $1,000 and $1,500 for a weeklong session; three vegetarian meals are provided.

**For More Information**   EastWest Retreats, 11780 San Pablo Avenue, 4C #304, El Cerrito, Calif. 94530; phone (510) 232-

3098; fax (510) 232-4090; e-mail: inservice@earthlink.com; Website: www.breathwork.com.

---

## JIMMY LESAGE'S NEW LIFE HIKING SPA
## Killington, Vermont

Fitness and nutrition expert Jimmy LeSage runs his hiking spa out of the Inn of the Six Mountains in the Green Mountains of Vermont. The spectacular scenery along trails surrounding the inn had attracted him; and after seeing that the ground could serve hikers of all levels of fitness, he knew that this would be the perfect place to create a lifestyle spa centered on the benefits of good nutrition and exercise outside in the fresh mountain air.

While vigorous morning walks are the focus of this spa experience, in the afternoons guests can choose from a number of fitness classes including aerobics, water aerobics in the outdoor pool, body toning, and yoga. Or they can treat themselves to spa amenities such as facials and therapeutic and relaxation massages. Also offered are biking, tennis, and golf.

Evenings are given to lectures on nutrition and lifestyle. Since there are no more than fifteen to twenty-five guests at any given time, everyone can be assured of one-on-one time with the expert staff.

**Season**    Early May to late October.
**Environs**    A cozy Vermont inn with hiking trails into spectacular Green Mountain scenery.
**Accommodations**    King-size or twin bedrooms with private bath.
**Activities and Services**    Hiking programs for all levels of fitness, outdoor pool, indoor lap pool, tennis, Jacuzzi, sauna, outdoor fitness pavilion.

**Religious Affiliation**   None.

**Rates**   The six-day/five-night Classic New Life Program is $999 (per person, single accommodations), or $899 (double); the four day/three-night Long Weekend is $599 (single), or $540 (double).

**For More Information**   Jimmy LeSage's New Life Hiking Spa, P.O. Box 395, Killington, Vt. 05751; phone (800) 228-4676; Website:www.killingtoninfo.com/iosm/newlife.htm.

―――――――

## KRIPALU CENTER FOR YOGA AND HEALTH
**Lenox, Massachusetts**

From its inception in 1957, the Kripalu Center for Yoga and Health has served as both a yoga ashram and a holistic life center. Its mission is to meld yoga and holistic medicine into a unified approach to physical, emotional, and spiritual health. All programs incorporate yoga several times a day as a clearing process to exhale and dispel physical, emotional, and mental blocks. Once freed of restraints, the mind and body can aspire to their unborn potential.

To help achieve that goal, sessions and classwork are focused and intensive. The accommodations are simple and the meals strictly vegetarian. Guests share dormitory-style rooms with bunk beds or spartan private rooms. There is no maid service, but linens and towels are replaced regularly. Meals are taken in silence.

The center attracts a wide range of age groups, from teens to the elderly. Special weeklong and longer programs address issues that are specific to each age range, such as Opening to Life After 50. Also addressed are issues that cross age boundaries such as illness, divorce, and other significant changes of life.

**Season**   Year-round.

**Environs**   The Berkshire Mountains of western Massachusetts.

**Accommodations**   Dorm-style housing (ten to twenty-four people per room), semiprivate rooms with shared or private baths, or private rooms with shared or private baths. Vegetarian meals are eaten in silence.

**Activities and Services**   Bodywork services including shiatsu, energy balancing, foot care/reflexology, meditative massage, and skin treatments (all for an added fee). Rising Phoenix yoga, yoga therapy. Saunas, whirlpools, private lake, communal meditation, and chanting.

**Religious Affiliation**   None.

**Rates**   Dormitory housing runs $70 to $80 per night, singles $140 to $195. Fees for a six-night workshop are $495 to $690 (dormitory), or $1,035 to $1,320 (single). Rates include three meals a day.

**For More Information**   Kripalu Center for Yoga and Health, Box 793, Lenox, Mass. 01240; phone (800) 967-3577.

---

## MOUNT MADONNA CENTER
## Watsonville, California

The Mount Madonna Center is a unique community gathered to nurture the creative arts and health sciences. Not a resort or spa, the site is a nonprofit center managed cooperatively by students of yoga inspired by teacher Baba Hari Dass. For the past twenty years, Mount Madonna has attracted renowned yoga instructors as well as the finest teachers and practitioners in the fields of health, healing, psychology, and dance. The breathtaking panoramic views of Monterey Bay have been no deterrent to the center's growing popularity.

When not engaged in the center's many culturally and spiritually enriching workshops, guests can enjoy miles of hiking trails, tennis, volleyball, and basketball. There is a gymnasium and hot tub as well as massage and herbal steam bath facilities. Meals are vegetarian.

The most recent addition to Mount Madonna is its conference center. Five hundred people can gather in the main lodge at one time and, while some may regret the crowds, the change was well worth it. By expanding the center's capacity for hosting programs and meetings, opportunities for learning have increased tenfold. Recent offerings include Art as a Way/Personal Shrines, Insight Meditation Practice, Polishing the Soul/Love and Creativity in Daily Life, and Mandala/Sacred Art of Transformation.

**Season**   Year-round.

**Environs**   The center is located on 355 mountaintop acres of redwood forest and meadows overlooking Monterey Bay; it's one hour from San Jose and two hours from San Francisco.

**Accommodations**   Single, double, triple, and dormitory rooms; camping is also available (bring your own tent). Meals are vegetarian, served cafeteria-style.

**Activities and Services**   Hiking trails, volleyball, tennis, basketball courts, gymnasium, small lake for swimming, hot tub. Massages and steam baths are available for a reasonable fee.

**Religious Affiliation**   None.

**Rates**   Call for rates. Some work-study scholarships are available.

**For More Information**   Mount Madonna Center for the Creative Arts and Sciences, 445 Summit Road, Watsonville, Calif. 95076; (408) 847-0406; fax (408) 847-2683; e-mail: programs@mountmadonna.org; Website: www.infopoint.com/orgs/mmc.

## MOUNTAIN TREK FITNESS RETREAT AND HEALTH SPA
## Ainsworth Hot Springs, British Columbia, Canada

Mountain Trek provides hiking adventures in a truly spectacular alpine setting. High in the mountains of British Columbia,
these retreats use clean air and exercise to expel big-city-living
toxins. Letting your breath go in this supportive environment,
you may also release worries and fears.

Excursions offered cater to beginning "gentle hikers,"
rugged "mountain warrior" types, and everyone in between.
Three guides hike with each group of no more than fourteen
guests each week. Since there are twenty to twenty-five different trails of varying levels of difficulty, you will never have
to hike the same one twice. Each day brings new terrain, new
views, and new experiences, as well as opportunities for
instruction in yoga or stretching (to improve your breathing
and avoid injury), and fifty-minute sessions of Swedish massage to work through any remaining muscle kinks. Of special
mention are a guided Herb Walk and a Llama Trek for animal
lovers. For an upper- and lower-body workout bonanza, try
the hiking-biking-kayaking combination adventure.

With all that Mountain Trek offers, it can be easy to forget
that the hot springs of Ainsworth are only a five-minute walk
away. Wonderful year-round, these springs are especially
refreshing in the winter months. That's when hiking at Mountain Trek turns to snowshoeing (cross-country skiing can be
substituted). Special dogsledding days are scheduled then as
well.

Natural, alternative medicine complements the scenery
well and is the focus of several Mountain Trek programs,
including a women-only Weight-Loss Week (supervised by a
naturopathic physician) and the resort's own Natural Health

Vacations. The former does not starve its guests, and it offers opportunities for pampering as well as reiki and color therapy. The Natural Health Vacations include supervised fasting, cleansing, and natural hygiene programs intended to promote preventative medicine and alternative health education. They too are opportunities for detoxification, rejuvenation, and weight loss.

**Season**   Year-round.

**Environs**   Thirty-four forested acres on the shores of Kootenay Lake, overlooking the Purcell Mountains in British Columbia; five minutes' walking distance from the hot pools at Ainsworth Hot Springs. Free shuttle service (Mondays and Fridays only) from Castlegar Airport, British Columbia; a one-hour flight from Vancouver or Calgary airports; or a four-hour flight from Spokane, Washington.

**Accommodations**   Twelve private bedrooms with private baths in a true mountain lodge with fireplace lounge; meals and snacks are provided.

**Activities and Services**   Hiking, snowshoeing, cross-country skiing (downhill and Snowcat skiing can be arranged at extra cost), yoga and stretching classes, Swedish massage. Facilities include an outdoor Jacuzzi, sauna, and gym with exercise studio, CYBEX-equipped weight room, and mini trampolines.

**Religious Affiliation**   None.

**Rates**   These vary per program and length of stay. The seven-night hiking program ranges from U.S. $1,560 to $1,825, the four-night hiking from $720 to $1,000. Programs (except for Natural Health) are all-inclusive of boarding, meals and snacks, daily personal laundry service, use of exercise clothes, bathrobes, backpacks, and water bottles, use of all facilities, complementary Swedish massage, and shuttle service from Castlegar Airport.

**For More Information**    Mountain Trek Fitness Retreat and Health Spa, P.O. Box 1352, Ainsworth Hot Springs, B.C. V0G 1A0 Canada; phone (800) 661-5161; phone/fax (250) 229-5636; e-mail: mtrek@hiking.com; Website: www.hiking.com.

---

## WHAT IS AROMATHERAPY?

In its broadest sense, aromatherapy is the use of the essential oils of plant leaves, flowers, and roots for healing. How exactly these oils are used can take many forms, from a massage with scented oils or a bath in infused mineral water to a body wrap. The oils have a fragrance that, when released into the air we breathe by rising steam, can clear our heads of congestion and our minds of worries.

Healing the mind and body through the use of essential oils and their fragrances may seem New Age but is in fact one of earliest forms of healing. So important were these treatments to early peoples that recipes for medicines, salves, and balms are some of our first recorded history. The Egyptians created fragrant oils from the bark of the cedar tree and released their aroma for rituals, celebrations, and healing. Recorded on papyrus are hundreds of herbal remedies and what they will cure. The Greeks went so far as to designate all aromatic plants as of divine origin and therefore sacred. During the Middle Ages and up until the end of the nineteenth century, perfume oils were valued as antiseptics able to protect the wearer from plague and death.

Over time the essential oils of various herbs, flowers, and roots have been analyzed and categorized by their healing effects on different parts of the mind and body. Slowly, modern science has come to see these oils as medical assets. Lavender oil, for instance, promotes healing of scar tissue, while cinnamon, oregano, thyme, and clove appear to strengthen the immune system.

The most popular use of aromatherapy in spa treatments is, however, to unwind. Ongoing studies are exploring the role essential oils can play in easing anxiety and stress, and possibly releasing us from depression. Anyone who has experienced the physical and emotional benefits of an aromatherapy massage or a calming sandalwood hydrobath knows how lucky we are that the ancients decided to pick up pen and papryrus and pass along some secrets otherwise held in the essences of nature's bounty.

## THE OAKS AT OJAI
**Ojai, California**

Nestled in the mountains just inland from southern California's rocky Pacific coastline, Ojai is a small town with an unpretentious character. The main street is only a block long, which makes finding the Oaks at Ojai a very stress-free way to begin a spa vacation.

The Oaks is known as an affordable fitness spa, with services attending to overall wellness and health. On the average day at Ojai, a guest has access to eighteen fitness classes ranging from light exercise to vigorous custom workouts. As part of its Stress Management Program, guests can enjoy expertly instructed yoga classes or take light strolls through the surrounding hills. For a more vigorous excursion into the mountains, Ojai guides offer an advanced six-mile hike. For a breather, try aqua-aerobics, a few laps in the pool, or a game of tennis. Spa cuisine is tasteful and usually weighs in at about one thousand calories a day. Special services highlight aromatherapy and include reflexology, reiki, facials, and exfoliating body treatments.

**Season**   Year-round.

**Environs**   A mountain retreat about twenty minutes north of downtown Ventura.

**Accommodations**   Private rooms, double lodge rooms, adjoining doubles, double cottages, and large triple cottages.

**Activities and Services**   Eighteen optional fitness activities, full-service spa, swimming pool, saunas, hot tub, weight training. Full-time nurse on staff for medical attention. Evening activities include cooking and nutritional lessons, arts and crafts workshops.

**Religious Affiliation**   None.

**Rates**   A private room including the daily program ranges from $200 to $215 per person per night. A variety of extended-stay options includes a five-night midweek package ($1,000 to $1,075); seven-night ($1,400 to $1,505); twelve-night ($2,400 to $2,580). Check on rates for accommodations in lodges and cottages.

**For More Information**   The Oaks at Ojai, 122 East Ojai Avenue, Ojai, Calif. 93023; phone (800) 753-6257; Website: www.oakspa.com.

-------

## STAR FOUNDATION RETREATS
## Geyersville, California

STAR (Self-Analysis Toward Awareness Rebirth) Retreats are for healing deep psychological and spiritual wounds. People come here on their own or at the recommendation of their therapists to get "unstuck," and to work more intensively on their core issues than regular talk therapy sessions allow. Though not a twelve-step program, it is said to complement one well. Therapies used vary from cognitive exercises to feeling work, art therapy, sand-tray therapy, and breathwork, the last of these being a very effective means of reaching far down into the psyche.

Retreats can last ten or fifteen days and are carefully structured to allow participants ample opportunity to work through their own particular issues without missing out on the interaction and camaraderie of a group experience. Each participant experiences one integrative breathwork session and one bodywork session intended to release chronically held pain or trauma. Since STAR Retreats deal with highly personal issues and can be psychologically and spiritually demanding, it's helpful to know that help is always on hand. The staff-to-guest ratio is nearly 1:1, including bodyworkers and retreat administrators who have each undergone the STAR program.

If an intense therapy experience is what you're looking for and STAR sounds appealing, be forewarned that it involves homework. Everyone must complete daily written assignments designed to help uncover and heal early decisions and negative experiences that may still exert a powerful influence in their daily lives.

**Season**　Retreats are scheduled for spring, summer, and fall.
**Environs**　Beautiful natural scenery. During 1999, retreats will be held at a 260-acre retreat center in Saratoga Springs in Upper Lake, California.
**Accommodations**　These vary depending on the retreat location.
**Activities and Services**　Individual and group therapy, bodywork, breathwork, art therapy.
**Religious Affiliation**　None.

**Rates**    Ten-day retreats costs $3,500, 15-day $5,200. This includes meals, shared accommodations, group and individual therapy sessions, and one bodywork session (two during a fifteen-day retreat).

**For More Information**    STAR Foundation, P.O. Box 516, Geyersville, Calif. 95441; phone (707) 857-3359; fax (707) 857-3764; e-mail: starfoundation@pobox.com; Website: www.starfound.org.

---

## VISTA CLARA RANCH
### Galisteo, New Mexico

This small retreat spa in the dry air and brilliant light of the Southwest brims with desert spirit. Known for birdsong and Anasazi-inspired sweat lodge ceremonies, Vista Clara offers terrifically inspirational group activities combined with some of the country's most personally attentive spa services.

Guest rooms are limited to ten, with the vastness of the landscape underscoring the aura of intimacy about programs and therapies. The archetype offering at Vista Clara is a half-day sweat lodge ceremony and feast to which everyone is invited. Other activities versed in Native American history, culture, and spirituality include horseback rides or hikes along rocky ridges etched with petroglyphs, and classes in Native lore. Popular among participants, these experiences are said to bring even the most untherapied among us out of our shells and into alliance with the physical and ethereal worlds.

Forget cooking demonstrations at large spa resorts; at Vista Clara, you can receive private cooking lessons from two celebrated southwestern chefs. Private art, jazz, and movement classes are also available. Body therapies range from the con-

servative Moor mud wrap to more adventurous treatments including lymph dry brushing, craniosacral therapy, reiki, and the ultimate: four-handed massage (this means two technicians at once!). Meals are both healthful and delicious, prepared from innovative spices and fresh produce native to the region—so fresh, in fact, that many ingredients are harvested in the ranch's own organic gardens and orchards.

**Season**  Year-round.

**Environs**   A high-desert retreat surrounded by mountains, about twenty-five minutes southeast of Santa Fe.

**Accommodations**   Rooms in southwestern decor with king or two double beds, each with private bath and balcony or private patio.

**Activities and Services**   Horseback riding, petroglyph hikes, sweat lodge ceremonies, music, art, and cooking classes. Facilities include sparkling ozone pools, outdoor ozone spa, and fitness center. A wide variety of spa treatments and evening lectures is offered.

**Religious Affiliation**   None.

**Rates**   All spa packages include lodging, meals, and snacks, use of all facilities, classes, daily hikes, lectures, sweat lodge ceremony, and transportation to and from Santa Fe. A five-night spa package averages $1,380 (per person, double occupancy); this price covers three massages, two body treatments, and one beauty treatment. A seven-night $1,950 package covers four massages, two body treatments, two beauty treatments, astrology reading or craniosacral therapy, and a horseback ride in Galisteo.

**For More Information**   Vista Clara Ranch, H.C. 75 Box 111, Galisteo, N.M. 87540; phone (888) 663-9772 or (505) 466-4772; fax (505) 466-1942; e-mail: vclara@newmexico.com; Website: www.vistaclara.com.

---

## ZEN MOUNTAIN MONASTERY
### Mount Tremper, New York

Maybe it's a Zen need for space that makes us climb mountains. At the least, higher ground can make us feel spiritually, as well as physically, elevated. Remote in the Catskills, this forested retreat is home to a true monastery, offering some very rigorous training in Zen principles and practices. Guests at Zen Mountain don't have to be interested in a Buddhist monastic lifestyle, but they do have to enter into the routine of the monastery while they're there. This includes walking meditation, chanting and bowing during services, and periods of caretaking work, which require absolute silence. And late risers beware. Days begin before dawn and end at about nine at night.

Retreatants can learn various forms of Buddhist meditation at Zen Mountain. Some, such as the silent form of Sesshin, are taught as seven-day or weekend intensives. Another scheduled offering, a Deep Listening Weekend, teaches retreatants mindfulness through breathing training, keeping a sound journal, and inventing musical instruments. Ikebana, the technique of Japanese flower arranging, is also taught here, as are martial arts. For the newcomer to Buddhist ways, the monastery offers a thorough Introduction to Zen Training course.

You may not reach Nirvana on Zen Mountain, but you can hope to experience some very fulfilling moments of stillness. All programs aim to provide participants with the skills and knowledge to integrate Zen practice into their daily lives. Results for some include increased abilities of concentration, stress reduction through disciplined breathing, breakthrough moments of creative thought and expression, and a strengthened will to affect their communities in a positive way.

**Season**   Year-round.
**Environs**   The monastery is located on 230 mountainous acres in a state forest preserve, bordered by the Beaverkill and Esopus Rivers. It's about one hundred miles north of New York City and eighty miles south of Albany.
**Accommodations**   Dorm-style housing (bring a sleeping bag

or blanket, towel, and loose, comfortable clothing). Private rooms are for monks, staff, and long-term program attendees only. Meals are mostly vegetarian and served buffet-style; retreatants are expected to help with the cleanup.

**Activities and Services**    Meditation instruction, bird-watching, haiku poetry workshops, miles of hiking trails, rock climbing, landscape painting, and t'ai chi.

**Religious Affiliation**    Zen Buddhist.

**Rates**    These depend on the program, but all are inexpensive.

**For More Information**    Zen Mountain Monastery, P.O. Box 197PC, South Plank Road, Mount Tremper, N.Y. 12457; phone (914) 688-2228.

# BODY-MIND LINGO

◆

*A Glossary for Newcomers to the Body-Mind Arts and Sciences*

**Abhyanga**   A panchakarma (Ayurvedic; see below) full-body herbalized oil massage, usually enacted by two practitioners.

**acupressure**   Acupuncture without needles, using instead the pressure of fingers and hands in specific locations on the body to unblock the body's energy flow to restore health and balance. (See also process acupressure.)

**acupuncture**   A process to open paths of energy that aid the body in healing; it uses special acupuncture needles to lightly puncture the skin, dissolving blockages of energy and restoring health.

**aikido**   Japanese martial art that employs holds and locks, using the principles of nonresistance in order to debilitate the strength of the opponent. It is practiced for sport and physical fitness, as well as for raising body awareness.

**Alexander Technique**   A program designed to increase the individual's conscious awareness and integration of movement, balance, posture, and intelligence. The emphasis is on learning to overcome harmful habits that may cause physical and emotional stress in the body, allowing daily activities to be performed more freely and efficiently.

**amma therapy**    Oriental bodywork focusing on the balance and free-flowing movement of chi (life energy) through the body. Amma therapists access chi energy channels through the tendino/musculature of the body and manual manipulation of energy points along the channels.

**aromatherapy**    The science of using essential oils (concentrated plant extracts) to treat the body, mind, and spirit through inhalation, topical application (massage, for instance), or ingestion (only under the guidance of a qualified medical professional). It is a more standardized profession in Europe, with roots in the ancient cultures of Egypt and India.

**asanas**    Yoga postures.

**Ayurveda (or Ayur-Veda)**    Ancient Indian folk medicine, literally translated as "the science of life." Much more than a medical science, it encompasses the spirit and soul with strong focus on dietary and lifestyle choices. It is recognized by the World Health Organization as an effective health science, and currently a research topic of the U.S. National Institutes of Health. (See also panchakarma chikitsa.)

**Ayurvedic shirodhara**    A five-thousand-year-old East Indian technique of massage in which hot herbal-scented oil is dripped from a suspended metal bowl onto your forehead, one drop at a time for up to twenty minutes, gradually increasing to a gentle stream.

**bioenergetic analysis**    Profiling an individual in terms of the physical, mental, and spiritual energy systems of the body. It combines therapy of the body and mind to help you solve emotional problems and raise your potential for joyful living.

**biofeedback** A method of monitoring body functions (such as brainwave patterns) using specially designed equipment. Its purpose is to train the body to create positive life changes by modifying certain activities without chemicals and their all-too-common side affects.

**body-oriented psychotherapy** Acknowledging the mind-body link, practitioners use a range of spa therapies (light touch, soft or deep tissue manipulation, breathing techniques, movement, or exercise) to help the psychotherapeutic process address emotional issues.

**centering prayer** Meditative Christian prayer using a sacred word (or words) and twenty-minute periods of silence to focus intention internally.

**chakra** The Sanskrit word for "wheel of light." There are seven chakras, or spinning energy centers, believed to generate the body's energy field.

**charismatic retreat** Christian healing retreat emphasizing personal religious experience and divinely inspired powers; it can involve praying in tongues and prophecy.

**chiropractic** A hands-on science aiming to manipulate the spinal column and nervous system into restored health without the use of surgery or drugs. The origins of the practice date to the ancient Egyptians, Hindus, Chinese, Babylonians, and Assyrians.

**circuit weight training** Exercise using weight-resistance equipment in an aerobic way.

**craniosacral balancing** The deeply relaxing and balancing rhythmic application of very light touch to the head, focusing on the cranial bones, the sacrum, and interconnected membranes.

**deep tissue massage**   Massage administered to affect the sub-layer of musculature and fascia. It requires a highly trained therapist with a thorough understanding of anatomy and physiology.

**enneagram**   An ancient circular diagram with nine points, believed to have mystical value.

**flotation therapy (or REST, Restricted Environmental Stimulation Technique)**   A process in which you lie on your side and float in less than a foot of salt water in a small, dark, enclosed chamber. This eliminates distracting stimuli of gravity, light, sound, and touch, and thereby leads to increased awareness, which can assist you in making physical and emotional changes.

**guided imagery**   Using mental images to affect changes in attitudes or behavior, including to promote physical healing. Its visualization exercises are especially helpful in alleviating stress or assisting in recovery from stress-related conditions.

**holistic health care**   Comprehensive and total care of a person's physical, emotional, social, and spiritual needs.

**holotropic breathwork**   Exercises for inner exploration based on modern consciousness research and ancient rituals. Breathwork can involve sessions of deep breathing, music, focused bodywork, and other activities to release energy.

**homeopathy**   Explaining symptoms as the outward effects of the body trying to overcome illness, homeopathic care treats "like with like" to facilitate the body in its own healing process. Thus it treats an illness with a substance that produces the same symptoms as those displayed by the person who is ill.

**hot-stone massage**   Therapeutic treatment combining massage with the soothing effects of contact with smooth basalt stones heated to over of 140°F in water.

**hydrotherapy** Water therapies including underwater jet massage, showers, jet sprays, and mineral baths.

**infant massage** A session in which qualified instructors teach parents how to safely and effectively massage their infants. Infant massage is successful not only in effecting critical weight gain in premature infants but also in creating a strong bond between parent and child and exposing the child to the benefits and pleasures of touch.

**kiatsu** Touch therapy with origins in the discipline of Aikido. Extending from a point in the lower abdomen, kiatsu therapists press perpendicularly toward the center of muscles to dispel tension, increase the flow of internal energy (chi or ki), and improve coordination of mind and body.

**kinesiology** The study of muscles in movement, the action of individual muscles, or groups of muscles that perform specific movements.

**kinesiology, applied** The practice of identifying imbalances of the energy fields within the body by examining the muscles. Once found, these energy imbalances can be corrected by specific massage techniques. Practitioners (many of them chiropractors) claim that this technique can relieve up to 80 percent of all human ailments as well as improve mental function, energy, mood, and overall happiness.

**light/color therapy** Using the different frequencies (or wavelengths) of light and color as quantifiable sources of energy. Variations in the effects of exposure to different frequencies on the eye affect muscular, mental, and nervous activity.

**lomi lomi massage** Traditional Hawaiian massage and healing technique. A form of lymphatic cleansing, it uses rhythmic rocking and the sound of chanting to relax your muscles and stimulate circulation.

**lymph drainage (or lymphatic massage)**   A gentle pumping massage technique that stimulates the lymphatic system to carry away pockets of retained water and toxins trapped in the loose connective tissue. It's noninvasive, painless therapy useful for individuals suffering swelling, neuromuscular disorders, and congestion; also considered by many a premier anti-aging treatment.

**mandala**   A ritualistic geometric design symbolic of the universe, used in Hinduism and Buddhism as an aid to meditation.

**meditation**   Any number of disciplined exercises to bring about relaxation and integration of body, mind, and spirit. In addition to promoting feelings of wellness, research has found meditation to alleviate medical conditions ranging from hypertension to asthma.

**mindfulness**   Buddhist term for the constant, nonjudgmental awareness of the moment and your place in it.

**Moor mud**   An organic Hungarian mud from the thermal lake at Herviz, famed for its detoxifying and exfoliating properties. It's used in various skin and beauty treatments.

**naturopathy**   The science of locating and ridding the individual of the origins of a disease, whether chemical, physical, or psychological. It works on the premise that the body has its own natural healing forces.

**ohashiatsu**   A form of bodywork intended to balance life energy (in body, mind, and spirit). It blends the healing techniques of Japanese shiatsu with the psychological components and teachings of Eastern philosophy.

**ortho-bionomy**   A form of hands-on bodywork that uses gentle movements and comfortable body positioning to unlock tension and relieve pain. It teaches people to be more at ease in their bodies, both physically and energetically.

**osteopathic medicine**   Physician-provided comprehensive medical care aimed at treating the patient as a whole person, rather than treating a disease or collection of symptoms. Many osteopaths (called D.O.'s) combine traditional Western methods with more natural or alternative treatments. All are specially trained in the art of manipulation—using their hands to diagnose, treat, and prevent illness.

**panchakarma chikitsa**   Ayurvedic treatments for detoxification and rejuvenation.

**polarity therapy**   Therapy aimed at releasing emotional tension or pain by restoring the body's natural flow of energy. It theorizes that positive and negative poles exist in every cell, and that the body can be gently manipulated to balance these positive and negative energies.

**process acupressure**   An integrative body-mind-soul approach that combines traditional acupressure techniques with process psychology skills to reclaim energetic balance in the body.

**qi gong (or chi kung)**   Oriental movement exercises promoting health, longevity, and a sense of harmony with origins in ancient India and China. From the word *qi* (*chi*) used to describe breath, vapor, air, and the internal energy, and *gong* (*kung*) meaning work, or achievement.

**reflexology (also called zone therapy)**   An ancient Chinese healing therapy that applies pressure with the thumb to reflex points on the feet, the hands, and, occasionally, the ears. With each touch, impulses are conveyed that cause a reflex response—thereby also stimulating body organs.

**reiki**   From the Japanese words *ray* for "divine wisdom," and *ke*, "life-force energy," this healing technique enhances the energy field that surrounds and penetrates the physical body. It was developed in the late nineteenth century by a Christian minister and teacher living in Japan and is now practiced with many nuances, all aiming to relieve the body of physical, emotional, and spiritual blockages.

**REST** (See flotation therapy.)

**Rolfing**   A series of deep muscle manipulations aimed at eliminating pain and restoring optimal posture.

**shiatsu massage**   Japanese bodywork technique that uses traditional Chinese acupuncture points. It applies rhythmic thumb, finger, and palm pressure, rather than needles, to acupuncture points in order to restore a more efficient flow of energy to the nervous system.

**shirodhara**   See Ayurvedic shirodhara.

**somatics**   A study of the self that involves focusing inward to witness and observe the minute and subtle movements of the body and its parts, from muscles and bones to organs and even cells. This field of study encompasses the disciplines of Rolfing, the Rosen Method, and the Feldenkrais Method.

**swedish massage**   A massage technique using five main strokes to stimulate blood circulation; it's based on the healing power of touch, which says that all strokes go toward the heart.

**Swiss shower**   Shower from powerful jets directed at the body from various heights; it has the effect of an invigorating massage.

**t'ai chi (or t'ai chi c'huan)**   The ancient Chinese discipline of meditative movement for the promotion of health and longevity; it helps raise awareness, stretch and tone the body, and improve the body's immune system.

**thalassotherapy**   From the ancient Greek *thalassa*, or sea, this term refers to spa treatments making predominant use of seawater, seawater plants, and sea air.

**therapeutic touch**   Using the hands to direct human energies to help or heal an individual suffering from illness (similar to the "laying on of hands").

**Trager bodywork**   A gentle and rhythmic massage technique designed to release tension and realign the body.

**transcendental meditation (TM)**   A technique of meditation derived from Hindu traditions that promotes deep relaxation through the use of a mantra.

**trigger point**   A location in the muscles that can be compressed to release tension and relieve pain, stiffness, loss of movement, inflammation, and sports-related injuries.

**vegan**   More than a vegetarian diet, vegan excludes the use or consumption of animal-based products (strict vegans do not eat honey or wear leather, for instance).

**VibraSound™**   A sensory resonance device designed to access different states of mind through light, sound, music, and vibration; it brings on an altered state that can result in intense feelings of pleasure.

**Vichy shower**   In this recumbent shower, you lie down on a waterproof cushioned mat and are doused from above by several jet streams.

**Watsu**   Short for *water shiatsu*, this technique combines Zen shiatsu with the experience of being gently floated and stretched in a warm pool of water (see the description of Harbin Hot Springs on page 125).

**yoga, Hatha**   *Ha* is Sanskrit for "sun," and *tha*, for "moon." Traditionally, these represent male and female energy. *Yoga* means "to yoke, or unify." Hatha yoga is therefore a discipline for integrating the opposing energies within an individual. It is generally taught as a system of postures and breathing exercises designed to improve health and prepare the body and mind for meditation.

**yoga, Kriya**   In this form of yoga, the emphasis is on a balance achieved through harmonizing the disparate parts of the mind into wholeness. A way of creative living, Kriya yoga teaches a type of meditation aimed at revealing the wisdom of life in daily experience.

**yoga, Kundalini**   Yoga as an energy management system, this form teaches awareness and improves health through exercises or postures (asanas), special breathing (pranayama), hand and finger gestures (mudras), body locks (bhandas), sound current (mantras), and meditation.

**yoga, Phoenix Rising**   Yoga infused with contemporary psychology, the purpose of which is dialogue. Assisted yoga postures and guided breathing causes a deep physical sensation whereby you can listen more closely to your body's wisdom and release underlying emotions or beliefs that typically manifest themselves as chronic pain.

**yoga, Sivananda**   A yoga system popularized by Swami Vishnu-Devan, this synthesizes the ancient wisdom of yoga into five basic principles for physical, mental, and spiritual health and self-realization: Proper Exercise, Proper Breathing, Proper Relaxation, Proper Diet, Positive Thinking, and Meditation.

# INDEX

$\blacklozenge$

## Alphabetical Index of Vacations

201

## Geographical Index of Vacations

## Topical Index

*The following list of program types and services is intended to help you find the vacation that meets your needs. While it does not list every fitness class, massage technique, and yoga variation, it does aim to represent the professional specialties and resort perks that can make a difference when choosing between destinations.*